"Brady Boyd's *Sons and Daughters* is ⸺⸺⸺⸺⸺⸺⸺⸺⸺⸺⸺.
We are all spiritual orphans seeking our way home in one way or another. In this book Brady shares moving stories, showing us that we are already accepted by God, enabling us to live both fearlessly and faithfully. I highly recommend this book to anyone seeking answers to living life more abundantly."

— MARK BATTERSON, Lead Pastor of National
Community Church in Washington, DC, and author
of *The New York Times* bestseller *The Circle Maker*

"I have long known Brady Boyd to be a man of deep spiritual insight and remarkable sensitivity to God's voice. I trust him. That's why I was not surprised to discover that *Sons and Daughters* is filled cover-to-cover with transformative glimpses of God's Father-heart for me (and you). I believe we live in a day in which most believers suffer to some degree from an 'orphan spirit.' Brady has not only penned a beautiful, biblical invitation to 'come home,' but has handed us a map that shows the way."

— KARI JOBE, Worship leader at Gateway Church
in Southlake, TX, and songwriter

"Having spent most of my childhood starved of the love and influence of an earthly father, the plight of orphans is very close to my heart. Brady Boyd's gentle and wise words about the transition from spiritual orphan to treasured child of God are like a healing balm for anyone who's ever longed for a place to call home."

— JIM DALY, President of Focus on the Family

"*Sons and Daughters* is liberating, educating, and motivating, an indispensable handbook for hope and health at a time when brokenness abounds. I could not put it down!"

— LYNETTE LEWIS, Corporate consultant, speaker,
and author of *Climbing the Ladder in Stilettos*

"Too many Christians believe the lie that says you have to earn God's grace. It is a free gift! Receiving that gift makes you a true child of an incredible Father. In *Sons and Daughters*, my friend Brady shows how you can stop living as a spiritual orphan and start living as a son or daughter of God. When you receive that revelation, it will change everything."

—ROBERT MORRIS, Senior Pastor of Gateway Church in Southlake, TX, and bestselling author of *The Blessed Life*, *From Dream to Destiny*, and *The God I Never Knew*

"This amazing book is a must read for all, but especially for those who struggle with their identity as a child of God. Brady Boyd captures you by the candid stories out of his own experiences and freeing insight."

— TOMMY BARNETT, Senior Pastor of Phoenix First Assembly and Co-founder of the Los Angeles Dream Center

"As pastors of Oasis Church in Los Angeles, my husband Philip and I find that we are half parents and half pastors to our congregation. It is an interesting place to be. Many in our church are in their twenties and thirties, looking for spiritual parents—which reflects an entire generation that hope to find their place and fulfill their purpose in history. In this book Brady Boyd takes us on a journey of receiving that all-important blessing from our Father. Rather than live as orphans, we can walk confidently into the future God has in store for us. I can't wait for our congregation to read it!"

—HOLLY WAGNER, Pastor of Oasis Church in Los Angeles and author of *GodChicks* and *Daily Steps for GodChicks*

"Brady Boyd presents us with a marvelously accessible, enjoyable, and practical procession of life-as-it-is anecdotes and applications that breathe truth, life, and refreshing. His lucid, grace-filled, and pungent style is at once touching, convincing, instructive, and inspiring."

— Jack W. Hayford,
Chancellor of The King's University – Los Angeles

"Brady Boyd explains the joy that comes from being a child of God and the frustrations that we all face. Through heartfelt testimonies of struggle and redemption, he shows just how precious it is to embrace our relationship with our heavenly Father. *Sons and Daughters* will challenge the reader to understand their place in the kingdom of God and why it is so important to fight for it."

—Pastor Matthew Barnett,
Co-founder of the Los Angeles Dream Center

SONS & DAUGHTERS

SPIRITUAL ORPHANS
FINDING OUR WAY HOME

BRADY BOYD

ZONDERVAN®

ZONDERVAN.com/
AUTHORTRACKER
follow your favorite authors

We want to hear from you. Please send your comments about this book to us in care of zreview@zondervan.com. Thank you.

ZONDERVAN

Sons and Daughters
Copyright © 2012 by Brady Boyd

This title is also available as a Zondervan ebook. Visit www.zondervan.com/ebooks.

This title is also available in a Zondervan audio edition. Visit www.zondervan.fm.

Requests for information should be addressed to:

Zondervan, *Grand Rapids, Michigan* 49530

ISBN 978-0-310-32769-1

Published in association with the literary agency Alive Communications, Inc., 7680 Goddard Street, Suite 200, Colorado Springs, CO 80920.

Cover design: Curt Diepenhorst
Cover photo: Lee Avison / Trevillion Images
Interior design: Katherine Lloyd, The DESK

Printed in the United States of America

12 13 14 15 16 17 /DCI/ 22 21 20 19 18 17 16 15 14 13 12 11 10 9 8 7 6 5 4 3 2

For Abram and Callie.
Forever and always.

✦✻✦

I will not leave you as orphans;
I will come to you.

— JOHN 14:18

CONTENTS

Foreword by John Eldredge 11

Acknowledgments 15

Introduction: I Just Want to Come Home 17

PART ONE: THE PATH TO SONSHIP   19

1. Frank 21

2. The Cry of the Orphan Heart 26

3. It Ain't about Money, and It Ain't about Sex 31

4. When an Orphan Becomes a Leader 34

5. How to Spot a Slave 39

6. Sinners Sin 44

7. How, Not What, I'm Doing 47

8. No Condemnation. Really 50

9. Mrs. Bright 57

10. Too Good to Be True 61

11. Who You Would Be, If You Chose to Live Free 65

12. Coming to Our Senses 68

13. A Son Who Knows He's a Son 73

PART TWO: LIVING WELL-LOVED   77

14. The Prayer of a Recovering Slave 79

15. Lone Cowgirl at a Princess Party 82

16. Lessons from Backwoods Tree Limbs 86

17. Monday-Morning Confessions
    from a Sunday-Loving Pastor 92

18. Disappointed with God 94

19. Heaven Breaking Through. 99

20. Epic Messes 102

21. Wave upon Wave of Love 105

22. The Difference between Soil and Dirt 110

23. On Fake Trophies and Bearing Fruit. 114

24. The Danger of Being at Our Best 119

25. The First Word of Every Good Prayer 123

26. A Plea to Young Pastors 128

27. Yuri Lite Star 133

28. Death to the Spinning Globe 137

29. Hype versus the Holy Spirit 141

30. Dad's Distinct Whistle 144

31. Sons and Daughters Lean In. 148

32. The Kingdom Is for Kids 153

33. Jesus Loves Me, This I Know 160

PART THREE: CARRIERS OF GRACE   **165**

34. Room for Both You and Your Burden 167

35. A Big Ol' Sloppy Helping of Grace 170

36. Untangled 174

37. First, a Heart of Compassion 177

38. Seeing Others for Who They Are 181

39. A Gun, a Hatchet, and a Horse 186

40. My Knobby-Kneed Peach Festival Girl 192

41. Humility, and How We've Perfected It. 195

42. For Freedom, We Are Set Free 200

43. In Favor of Inconvenience 203

44. The High Stakes of Sonship 208

45. Fathered Sons Father Well 213

46. On Responding, Retaliating, and Setting
    the Record Straight 217

47. The Purpose of Forgiveness 225

48. The Jonah Syndrome 231

49. Biscuits and Gravy, with a Side of Silence 235

50. To Smell of Bourbon and Smoke. 238

51. Forever and Always Family 244

52. Here Lies a Grateful Sheep. 247

    Afterword 251

    Notes 253

FOREWORD

One of my favorite quotes from the old Scottish pastor George MacDonald is this: "Because we are the sons of God, we must become the sons of God."

I love this quote because it is both an affirmation and an invitation.

The affirmation is simple and profound: we *are* the sons and daughters of God. Those of us who have placed our faith in Jesus Christ and welcomed him into our hearts are now — and forever will be — children of our Father God. Oh, may our souls rest in this unchangeable fact: We belong to God; we are family now. And nothing ever can take this away. That is the affirmation, and I feel as if I ought to repeat it to myself every day — write it on my bathroom mirror, my computer screen, my hand. I am a son of God, I am a son of God, I am a son of God.

Now, the *invitation* is just as profound, but not nearly so simple: to *become* a son or daughter. This involves a process that changes the way we see ourselves, the way we see others, the way we relate to God and to our world. We need the invitation because, truth be told, most of us don't live like that. Even though we are sons and daughters, we still perceive ourselves and our lives through a very different set of lenses.

Why, for so many years, would I wake up in the morning with the urgent feeling that, *I've got to get going; I've got to get on top of things*? I would hit the floor running, and I'd run all day long. Even if externally things didn't appear that way, inside, they definitely were. *Gotta answer those emails, gotta get that project done.* Time with God felt like a luxury, checking in with friends a colossal inconvenience.

Pushing a bit deeper into the truth of it, my basic reaction to disappointment was this: *I knew it.* A flat tire, a bounced check, a vacation we couldn't take after all — I met every disappointment with a posture in my soul that essentially said, *I knew it. If I don't make it happen, it isn't going to happen.* I can't say that I was expecting blessing; I expected hassles, frustration, distress.

On a relational level — which is the truest barometer of how we are living, by the way — why is it that for too many years it was just too hard for me to make friendships work? I had dozens of acquaintances and colleagues but very few genuine friends. Part of the reason was the drivenness I described above *(I've got to get on top of things).* You can't have friends if you're running all the time. But another part of the reason had to do with an emotional detachment I adopted a long time ago, a basic life commitment of, *I don't need you.* It was a self-protective strategy born out of disappointment and heartache, one which you may have adopted yourself, even if you've never admitted it.

Even years and years into my Christian life, the ways I interpreted an event, a comment, an email, or a setback did not jibe with the settled confidence of a well-loved son but rather reflected the emotional posture of an orphan. Though I *am* a son of a loving Father, I wasn't really living like one. Not emotionally, not in the way I did life, not in the way I reacted to things.

That's why I said yes when my friend Brady asked me to write this foreword. People need this book. *I* need this book. In fact, moments after I received the request, I thought, *I need to* read *this book, not contribute to it.* I'm still an infant in these matters; the longest strides I've taken toward sonship have been only in the last six months. But I now see Jesus was in Brady's invitation, just as he is in your choice to pick up this book. He is inviting us to go deeper into becoming a son or daughter. And the invitation is worth saying yes to. Of that much, I am sure.

My father passed away last summer. Though it was a sad moment, it was, frankly, a little anticlimactic. You see, in one sense my father has been dying for the better part of forty years. First it was the alcohol, then the stroke, then cancer. The man had a hard life. As a result, so did I. During those fatherless years, I developed a very independent approach to life. I took on the consciousness I mentioned above: *I've got to get on top of things; if I don't make it happen, it isn't going to happen; I don't need you.* The emotional and psychological outlook of an orphan, through and through.

But since Dad's passing, something has begun to shift inside.

Maybe it took the stark experience of spreading my father's ashes in the Snake River to make me face the fact that I am fatherless. *Now what will I do?* Maybe his passing made room in my soul for the ache for a Father to come to the surface. Maybe it was just the timing of God. For whatever reason, finally I feel like I have accepted the invitation to *become* a son more sincerely than I ever did before. I would describe it as one of the greatest episodes of my life — I am finally becoming a son. And with it, all sorts of cool things are happening.

I no longer feel that compelling pressure to get on top of things; I don't live with that awful burden that life is up to me. I wake up in the morning with some breathing room. My friendships feel more spacious, too, like they can go deeper now. And I am actually coming to expect love and blessing from God as the major theme of my life, not just bracing myself for the hassles of an undeniably broken world. Not all the time, not every day, but with greater and greater consistency, my soul feels more at rest these days, and it is changing the way I react to pain, to disappointment, and to loneliness. Wow! I am really becoming a son.

So my prayer for you is simply this: May Jesus open your heart and soul to see the ways you are still living as what Brady calls a "spiritual slave" or a "spiritual orphan"; may he help you realize the many ways it is affecting your relationships, your work, your ministry, your life. And may Jesus lead you to the grace of *becoming* a son or daughter, lead you to the healing love of your Father, give you the grace to accept a whole new way of approaching your life.

You are a child of God; now you get to become one.

—John Eldredge

ACKNOWLEDGMENTS

The single greatest joy I have on this earth is being the father to Abram and Callie and the husband to Pam. Many of this book's stories grew from the fertile soil of their hearts. It is an unspeakable joy to watch a young man and a young woman grow into a true spiritual son, a true spiritual daughter—and to watch their mom, my bride, Pam, as she brings the peace and presence of spiritual daughter with her throughout the course of her every day. She carries it better than any woman I have ever met and is a treasure from heaven to me and to all who know her.

Immeasurable thanks go to my mom and my late dad, Pat and Leland Boyd, for calling "son" out of me and giving me ample room to thrive under their care. You believed in me when I did not believe in myself, and you sacrificed more on my behalf than anyone ever will know.

Thank you, Ashley Wiersma, for catching the real spirit of this book and for crafting words and sentences that wound their way into life-giving chapters. I see "daughter" in every part of your life.

Thank you, New Life Church, for accepting me, loving me, and allowing my little tribe to be a part of your family.

Thank you, Pastor Tom Lane, for being my spiritual dad. Besides my own father, you have taught me more about fatherhood than any other person on the planet. You are the best dad I know.

Thank you, Pastor Clark Whitten, for your revelatory teachings on grace. At a men's retreat many moons ago in Buena Vista,

Colorado, you taught for three straight days on the subject, and it was then that my journey toward sonship began.

Thank you, Jesus, for adopting me. Because you did, we are now friends. Forever and always.

I JUST WANT TO COME HOME

I n the 1930s, a fourteen-year-old girl came home one afternoon and broke the news to her father — a stern, dogmatic, religiously churchgoing man — that she was pregnant. As the story goes, his reaction was no surprise to her. She had seen him this angry before. But being disowned at fourteen? Where was she supposed to go?

Believing no other option was available to her, she traveled from her home in Baton Rouge, Louisiana, to the city of New Orleans, eighty miles south. *Maybe I can find work there*, she figured. Surely something would pan out.

The streets of New Orleans were no place for a young teen. Alone, scared, desperate for a way out of her pain, she birthed her baby and jumped at the first job she could find. Prostitution is not a glamorous path, but it proved lucrative for the now-fifteen-year-old mom. Not only did she become good at the job; she became a smart, savvy businesswoman too. Years later she would own her own brothels and die with more money than she ever could have spent, had she lived another lifetime more.

On her deathbed, the frail and failing woman plotted the tombstone she desired for her grave. On it was etched a replica of the large front porch of her childhood home, with a young teenage girl peeking through the front window. Below the image were six searing words that summed up her wayward life: "I just want to come home."

Today she is buried in a small country cemetery in a southern Louisiana town. She lived and died and never knew what it felt like to be welcomed home.

My brother was traveling through Louisiana, my family's home state, when he found that woman's grave. He told me the story of her tragic life—a story that has been passed down for generations as part of Louisiana folklore—and still I can't shake it from my mind. If only she had learned of grace, divinity's ever-ready embrace.

There has never been a prodigal so far off that God's reach didn't stretch farther still. What healing and hope we find in the One who points orphan feet toward home.

PART ONE

THE PATH TO SONSHIP

We all start out as orphans on the mighty seas of life.
Alone. Afraid. All too aware
  that we're in way over our heads.
Captains of our own souls!
Desperate not to sink.
Rescue reaches down, points us
  toward All Is Well.
If only we'd believe there is a course that leads us home.

1

FRANK

The most unmistakable spiritual orphan I have ever known is a
man named Frank with whom I did ministry when I lived in
Texas. Frank was the kind of driven fortysomething man who pursued every high-capacity job that became available and constantly
scrutinized the church's organizational chart to determine how
many boxes separated him from the top. He was irrationally consumed with proving himself, but it would be many months into
our relationship before I'd learn why.

Frank was one of my direct reports, and each week he and I
would convene for a one-hour oversight meeting. The purpose of
our get-together was for me to help troubleshoot any major challenges he was facing in his role, and for him to update me on the
critical issues unfolding in the various ministries he oversaw. But
despite my clarifying these objectives numerous times, Frank used
the meetings as opportunities to garner my praise by exhausting
me with his good work. Each week, he would sit down across
from me in my office, lean forward in his chair, and plunk down
a thick clutch of papers with meticulously typed, single-spaced
notes, questions, and concerns covering both front and back of
each page.

Once he had the floor, he would start at the top of page 1 and work his way down to the bottom of the last side of the last sheet, and by that point I would be as badgered and beat as an at-home mom with eight kids. I appreciated Frank's thoroughness, but anyone who spends 20 percent of his time doing his job and the other 80 percent covering his rear end in case he happens to make a mistake is not going to last long on my team. Frank was dutifully following all the rules, but his leadership lacked intuition and strength.

After several of these agonizing sessions, I decided the madness must end. I explained to Frank that the following week I wanted him to come to our meeting with no more than three key discussion points and that I expected him to tackle his everyday work on his own. "Focus less on trying to prove yourself, Frank, and more on effectively leading your team."

Several months after our conversation, he still continued to struggle. Not just on the leadership front but also relationally. He seemed distrustful of his colleagues, even angry from time to time. A staff member would innocently question Frank about a particular ministry initiative, and Frank would erupt in frustration, as though that person were challenging Frank's character.

Finally, after a half-dozen of his emotional eruptions, I knew something had to give. I knew that I had an orphan spirit on my hands and that his only hope for healing was to walk the path toward "son." I called Frank into my office and said very calmly, "Listen, either you will get healthy, or I will fire you. Your behavior is bordering on abusive, and there is no place for abuse in this culture. Our people are too precious to be treated this way. And you are too precious to continue refusing help."

Grudgingly, Frank agreed to be led through a series of small group ministry sessions that teach biblical methods for breaking free from strongholds such as anger issues or addictions and invite people into the abundance Christ offers his followers. During his group's first session, Frank was asked to tell his story, beginning with his early childhood years.

Frank grew up with an alcoholic father who abandoned him and an impoverished mother who then gave him away. "I grew up in an orphanage," Frank explained. "My mom had abdicated her parental rights, and so I spent my entire childhood holed away in a children's home, waiting for a family to stop in that might want a kid like me."

Every other Saturday, Frank and all of the other discards would take baths, dress in their best clothes, and stand nervously in a line in the common area as prospective parents entered the building and looked them over. "At three and four years old, I was small for my age—scrawny even," Frank said. "To make matters worse, I had terrible eyesight. I wore Coke-bottle glasses with thick black frames, and twice a month, just like clockwork, I was overlooked by those moms and dads, all of whom wanted a 'normal' child." Frank was the smelly, mangy mutt at the kennel that nobody wants to take home.

When Frank was five, an older kid in the orphanage began sexually abusing him. "I didn't know what he was doing," Frank explained, "but I knew that it hurt and that I didn't like it at all." Frank summoned some courage and privately approached his houseparent with the facts: one of the older boys was doing something to him that was painful and upsetting, and something should be done to make him stop. The houseparent looked into the eyes of that wounded five-year-old and said, "You mustn't make up stories like that, Frank. Now run along and play."

At this point in the freedom ministry session, Frank looked at me and said, "Brady, I made a vow as a five-year-old that people weren't to be trusted and that I'd never have a place to belong." Frank had carried those orphan agreements with him for three-plus decades too long.

One Saturday when Frank was eight years old, a couple entered the orphanage and decided that among all the children, they liked Frank best. They told the houseparent to have Frank ready for pickup the following weekend and that they would return at a designated time to take him home. Frank spent the week floating on the clouds.

The following Saturday, after putting on his only pair of dress slacks and a button-down shirt, Frank perched himself on the threadbare couch in the home's main entryway, figuring he shouldn't risk missing his new parents when they arrived. Frank stayed in that seat through breakfast, lunch, and the handful of bathroom breaks he needed but refused to take, until finally, late that afternoon, one of the houseparents came to Frank and said, "Listen, son, they're not coming."

Frank was dumbfounded. "But they said that they would be here!"

In the end, the couple craved a daughter. And the unwanted mutt remained flat on the kennel floor.

Frank slunk back to his room, where he undressed and put on his play clothes, and then sat in stunned silence the rest of the day.

When Frank turned eleven, another couple showed interest in the young boy. Hesitant to believe he really might be chosen, he hedged his bets and kept his expectations low. But two Saturdays later the couple returned, helped Frank pack his bags, and took him home to live with them. Adopted at last — by a family to call his own.

During Frank's sophomore year of college, he surrendered his life to Christ and began studying to become a pastor. But he never dealt with the orphan spirit that had been hardwired in his soul. He knew all the right things to think; he just couldn't transport them to his heart. Frank bore out what I have consistently found to be true: spiritual orphans are the easiest people to point toward faith in Jesus Christ but the most difficult to disciple. They say yes to family, but they have no idea how to walk out the realities that new relationship affords. They desperately want to belong, but once they are given a seat at the table, they decline dinner day after day. They don't believe that God really wants them around, that he's actually *excited* to call them his own.

But that's exactly what Ephesians 1 says about God, that he is brought great "pleasure" when we live as his daughters and sons. We bring our Father divine delight when we approach him confidently, trust him deeply, seek him intently, and are clear about the worth of our role.

We all start out as Franks in this world, believing we are unseen, unwanted, and unloved. But by God's grace, we don't have to stay there. We don't have to stay orphans for long.

2

THE CRY OF
THE ORPHAN HEART

Last year, the pastor of our ministry to college students, Aaron Stern, invited fifty-five mature men who are devoted followers of Jesus Christ to one of the group's weekly gatherings. Toward the end of the worship service, Pastor Aaron asked his wife and four young sons to join him onstage, and in front of more than a thousand college students that evening, he prayed a prayer of blessing over each of his boys. With loving arms wrapped around them, he thanked God for his sons' unique personalities and spiritual gifts. He affirmed his boys for wanting to make choices that honor God and for being such a delight to their parents. He prayed for God's will to be done in their lives. He prayed for their safety, for their protection, for their provision, for their peace. And then he went down the line, placing his hands on each boy's shoulder, saying, "You're a great son! I love you, and I'm thankful for you. I bless you in the name of Jesus Christ. And here tonight, I want to tell you that your mom and I are *pleased* with you. We are *for* you. And we can't wait to see what God continues to do in and through your life."

The room was silent for several minutes as the group took in what they had just seen. Pastor Aaron then looked at the eyes staring back at him from the crowd and said, "I know many of you have never had a dad pray for you like that. You've never had someone you look up to say they love you and are thankful for you and are pleased with who you are becoming.

"You've never had a dad lovingly lay hands on your shoulders and say he's on your side. You've never been encouraged in this type of meaningful way.

"And so," he continued, "I decided that tonight, that ought to change."

The fifty-five men — some elders, some staff, all members of New Life Church — were then invited to come to the front of the room and form an arc around the stage. "If you have never received a prayer of blessing from a father," Aaron said, "these men are ready to serve you tonight. Come down front, shake hands with one of them, and let them hug you and pray over your life."

As soon as the service was dismissed, the room tipped over as hundreds of young men and women crowded the altar, their faces stained with tears. Some of those kids went through the line and received prayer, only to get back in line again. They were sponges soaking up long-awaited care. They were orphans trying to come home.

❧

If you were to put your ear to the ground of modern culture today, you would hear the agonized cries of an orphan heart: *Doesn't anybody notice me? See me? Value me? Want me? Is there anywhere for me to belong?*

I'd be willing to bet that easily more than half of our population has never had an earthly father place his hands on their shoulders and with warmth and sincerity pray a prayer of blessing over their lives. They have never once heard the words, "You are my son ... my daughter ... and I *delight* in you." They have never known the feeling of truly being seen, of being loved. Of being cheered on in the same way that God affirmed his own Son.

Just before Jesus began his public ministry here on planet Earth, he chose to be baptized by John, as a way of letting onlookers know that he was devoted to following his heavenly Father's will rather than going the world's way with his life. Matthew 3 says that "as soon as Jesus was baptized, he went up out of the water. At that moment heaven was opened, and he saw the Spirit of God descending like a dove and alighting on him. And a voice from heaven said, 'This is my Son, whom I love; with him I am well pleased'" (vv. 16–17).

That single verse of Scripture launched the most impactful season of ministry the world ever has known, and confirmed for all eternity that Jesus was no orphan. He was no slave. He was God's one and only *Son*. And with him God was *pleased*.

Do you know how drastically the crime rate in the United States alone would drop if *all* children grew up knowing they were pleasing to their dads? Do you know how precipitously the divorce rate in this country would fall if every boy, every girl, grew up knowing he or she was precious to an earthly dad? Do you know how much pain could be spared if we could just get this one thing right?

I think the answer would stagger us both.

✦✧✦

I remember like it was yesterday the season of my dad's death. His health had been declining steadily, and one night, there in the small living room of my parents' house, I sat beside my highly medicated father as he reclined on the couch. He was in and out of coherence, so I tried to time my comments with his more lucid moments. At one point, I caught his eye and said, "Dad, you have been a great father to me. You really have." I told him what I valued most about his parenting and about his friendship, and I expressed to him what I would miss most once he departed this earthly life. Nearly every day of my life, my dad had told me that I was smart, that I was talented, that I could be anything I wanted to be. He told me that he was proud of me, that he was pleased with me, and that he loved me more than I ever would know. I knew no limitations to my capability, because in Dad's eyes, I could fly. No one else would ever love me exactly the way my dad did.

I looked into my frail father's eyes and said, "You know, the only thing I would ask of you is that you would pray a prayer of blessing on my life. You have been so affirming through the years, but you've never laid hands on me and prayed for me. ... It would mean so much to me if you would do that, Dad."

I'm not sure how I expected my father to respond, but seeing him convulse with waves of tears was nowhere on the list. I had never seen my dad cry uncontrollably, never heard guttural moans like that. In an attempt to quell his tears, I reiterated the positives. "Dad, you got fathering so right! You are an *amazing* dad, and I love you deeply. All I want you to do is to lay hands on me and pray for me. I just need to hear the words of a prayer like that from my one and only dad."

Still, he couldn't do it. I don't know if it was the emotion of the moment or his grave situation in general or that he simply didn't know what to say; all I know is that I never received that prayer.

That evening, realizing I never would be given my father's blessing, I laid my hands on his shoulders and blessed him instead. "Lord, I thank you for Dad," I said. "I thank you for his life and for his legacy. I love this man, and I feel overwhelming gratitude for having been placed in his family as his son. I know he is pleasing to you ... and he is pleasing to me too."

I asked God to relieve my dad's ever-increasing physical pain, I asked him to heal the disease that was ravaging his body, and I prayed that he would assure my dad of a life well lived, a home well led, a family well loved. Tears continued to stream down my father's face as I embraced him that night. That brief time of prayer remains one of the most meaningful memories I carry of my dad.

⌣

Most people I meet who are plagued by an orphan spirit believe that Jesus Christ can save them; they just can't seem to fathom how he enjoys them too. It's interesting, isn't it? The cry of the orphan heart is, *Won't somebody please see anything remotely worthwhile in me?* And all the while God lovingly says, *I do. I really do.*

Every weekend at New Life, as I am dismissing the service, I ask our congregation to take time before they leave to introduce themselves to two or three people they do not know. It's not just a fleeting comment; there is deep purpose behind my reminder. What goes through my mind as I say those words is, *Please, New Life, do what I'm asking you to do. Please let God lead you to a possible divine encounter. The power of even a passing word can radically change a life.*

Countless people sitting in our auditorium every weekend carry an orphan spirit. They are unimpressed by flashy lights, loud surround sound, and the slightly above-average speaker on the stage. What impresses them — what really *moves* them — is to be seen. To be acknowledged. To be greeted. To be embraced. To be cared for and prayed for and loved.

God knows it's what moves us all. He knows that's what brings us home.

3

IT AIN'T ABOUT MONEY,
AND IT AIN'T ABOUT SEX

Given what I do for a living, I get a steady stream of folks through my office who look to me to help fix whatever is broken in their lives. I have met with men, women, couples, teenagers, believers, people living far from God, people who believe there is *no* God, and more. Their problems have run the gamut of troubling issues: drug addiction, alcohol addiction, adultery, strife. Bitterness and anger and depression and grief. Marriage troubles, parenting troubles, troubles with bosses and friends. Investments gone bad and bank accounts dried up and job loss and foreclosure and pain.

They are wounded, worried, and weak, and wonder how to right all that is wrong. And it's with shoulders slumped from all this weight that they step into my office and sit down.

A frustrated man and a weary woman are seated across from me, the looks on their faces begging me to glue back together the shattered fragments of their marriage. He was raised by an alcoholic father and a distant mother; she was raised by combative parents who largely led separate lives. Neither of them was shown how to give love, how to receive love, how to contribute to health in the home. It was against this distressing backdrop that they said their heartfelt "I dos."

They come to the end of themselves quickly, and within years he is accepting false love via a pornography addiction, and she is soothing her need to be seen by funding the latest clothing trends with money they do not have. Now they are in my office. "Fix us!" their countenances scream.

Certainly, debilitators such as overspending and porn need to be acknowledged, addressed, and resolved. But these are merely symptoms of root problems, which lie deeper still.

I have spent the past decade dissecting what God says about who we are—and about *what* we are, once we surrender our lives to him. We are new and alive and blessed and free, righteous and holy and redeemed. We are joyful, prayerful, purposeful, thankful, and eternally positioned with Christ. We are called overcomers, victors, ministers and saints, heirs and believers and friends. But the most compelling role I have been able to find is that of God's *daughters and sons.* If you were to unravel the fabric of my heart, the thematic thread you would be holding in your hands would be this: Getting clear on our *identity*—and that alone—is what determines how well we will live.

✠

My contention is that the vast majority of Christ followers do not understand who they are. They can talk for hours about what they do, who they know, where they've been, and the struggles they've overcome in this life. But when it comes to *who they are*, the conversation falls flat. We agree superficially that we are "God's children," even as we live like orphans and slaves. We control and perform and manipulate and strive all to secure a place where we can belong, and in so doing, thumb our nose at the idea that God holds us safely in his hand.

If I could offer one word of encouragement to the hurting people I come across—people like that couple struggling to find intimacy again; people, perhaps like you, who may also wrestle with *who they really are*—it would be this: take God at his word. That's it. *Take God at his word.* Be set free from tightfisted religion and from deception in all its tragic forms and rest in the secure knowledge that you are accepted and loved by God. Let his abundance be enough for you, instead of thrill-seeking your days away.

We can watch our lives be put back together again, regardless of what we have done. We can know wholeness and holiness and hope, instead of settling for brokenness and pain. We can walk closely with One who will never cast us aside, who will envelop us with unconditional love. We can be freed from the things that have bound us, that have convinced us we will always be caged.

We can. You can. *I* can, I know. I've seen it happen firsthand in my life.

◆≍◆

Over the twelve months that I spent writing this book, friends and colleagues asked me what I hoped to accomplish in these pages. My answer is always the same. "I've been on a journey of discovery," I explain, "and it's one I wish everyone would take." By stepping onto the path called sonship, every spiritual slave can find freedom, and every spiritual orphan can finally come home. This single revelation changes *everything*. It's why I am so passionate about this book.

I am not asking you to memorize a complex religious formula that promises to revolutionize your world. I am not asking you to pray a prayer, recite a creed, walk an aisle, attend a conference, join a church, lead a small group, or get dunked in a baptism pool. What I am asking you to do is *believe*. You are a son or a daughter of the most high God, the one who spread out the heavens and who numbers the hairs on your head. *That* God—he is the one who calls you his own. Your part, then, is to believe you have a prized place in his family and to live as though that belief is true.

Because it is.

4

WHEN AN ORPHAN
BECOMES A LEADER

Several years ago I agreed to consult with a church whose senior pastor had unexpectedly resigned. It wasn't a very civil departure, and the leaders who remained needed help picking up the pieces and moving into a future that would be brighter than their past.

I first met with the pastoral staff, the five or six key men and women who had been closest to the pastor who had left. "Tell me about the leadership culture here," I said, a request I thought was benign. The tales that spilled out broke my heart. So it goes when you work for a spiritual orphan, as these people obviously and unfortunately had.

When orphans become leaders of anything—a ministry, a small group, a business, a family—they can't help but harm everyone they lead. To a spiritual orphan, love is a weapon, to be wielded or withheld at will. They extend love when it serves them well, and they quickly withdraw it when it doesn't. Never having learned how to relate in a fluid and predictable manner, they appear erratic in their attitudes and behaviors. They can kill you with kindness Monday morning, only to wound you with their words that afternoon. They create in their leadership culture the orphan spirit they've carried their entire lives.

During my interviews with the pastoral staff, I learned that their former boss fit the orphan profile to a T. Because he himself wrestled with having a place to belong, he instilled this same insecurity in the hearts of people he led. His staff never knew if they were accepted or if they were passing muster with him, even as they worked long hours and devoted themselves to their jobs. Instead of communicating directly with his team, this leader would talk in code. "Read my silence," he would say on countless occasions. "It speaks *far* louder than my words." You can imagine the emotional damage this did to a team that really wanted to please their boss. After each leadership meeting, they would spin their wheels for hours, trying to decipher what, exactly, had been "said."

To make matters worse, this leader deceived everyone who knew and loved him. To clarify, lying is giving false information purposefully; deceiving is giving false information that you actually believe is true. It would take this team many focused months to untangle the knots their leader had tied. His baggage had become their baggage. His war had become their war. And this, even though part of a leader's responsibility is to *protect* the people he's entrusted to lead. I will never forget the deadened gaze of those pastors who had been spiritually abused. When orphans become leaders, irreparable damage always is done.

✳

Soon after Communism's fall in Romania in 1989, the watching world was stunned to learn of state-run orphanages overflowing with neglected kids. Under Romania's leadership at the time, both contraception and abortion were forbidden, causing a spike in unwanted pregnancies. The babies born during that era were relegated to bleak housing that lacked adequate washing and medical treatment facilities. What's more, the nannies' answer to keeping the young children quiet and in line often involved abuse—both physical and sexual—and even the administration of illegal drugs.

Much has changed for the better in Romania since those dark and derelict days—children are being reunited with their birth parents, they are entering trustworthy foster care, they are being adopted within the borders of Romania, and they are being invited into the safety of qualified group homes. But this happened only after worldwide outcry demanding action for these curb-kicked kids. And finding shelter in the arms of a loving family is only step one on a long journey toward healing and health.

As the realities of life in a Romanian orphanage surfaced, scientists began to study what happens when an orphan stays an orphan far too long. In one case, a leading researcher took a group of visitors to see one of the orphanages that was being shut down, and immediately a seven-year-old girl ran up the path to greet them, her arms outstretched as though wanting one of the strangers to pick her up. The translator yelled for the visitors not to touch her, but one of the group's members already had. Rather than curling into the embrace, though, the young girl stood erect like a tree trunk, not comforted by the contact in the least.

The problem, the researcher later explained to the group, was not the actual contact. It was that, at some point, the contact had to come to an end, and as soon as that little girl was released from the embrace and the group was out of sight, she would beat her head against the pavement as a means of dealing with the rejection she had just faced.

Without significant intervention, the girl would grow up with a severely flawed self-concept and deep suspicion toward all humankind.

In another case, the same researcher studied three boys who entered one orphanage as babies. He was showing a colleague of his a video he had filmed of the boys playing outside the main building, when he asked, "Looking at the boys' size, how old do you take them to be?"

The colleague guessed five, maybe six, years old. As it turned out, the boys were all eighteen. "Growth stunting," the researcher explained. "Not from lack of nutrition, but simply from lack of love."[1]

The theory that emerged from that scientist's studies was that growing up in a highly stressful environment, such as a place where babies receive no attention from adults, prohibits the body from producing adequate growth hormone. Countless kids couldn't find a way to thrive in the face of deprivation like that.

But take these same abandoned children and connect them with parents who care, and in a matter of not years or decades but *weeks* they begin to baby-step their way toward health. They grow taller. They grow stronger. Their minds grow sharper. They learn to love. One researcher's summary states, "The bottom line is kids do best in families, whether created through birth, adoption or foster care. Institutions can't provide the individual attention and stimulation of normal family life."[2]

✢✢✢

I shared these findings with the pastors from that church whose leader had left, to substantiate my point, namely, that when orphans become leaders, they can't help but harm everyone they lead. And while their leader had never been a physical orphan, the spiritual signs formed a direct parallel to the issues and insecurities orphans often face. He couldn't handle rejection — even *perceived* rejection — well. Although he led a large staff and an even larger church, his personal growth was drastically stunted in many areas — so when it came to giving and receiving love, he tended to be manipulative.

But just as those Romanian orphans who had finally been placed in safe, steady families eventually emerged as healthy daughters and sons, so too could these pastors choose to break the orphan spirit's claim on their lives. They could band together as family. They could be genuine in their love toward one another and toward the church at large. They could be consistent in their leadership. They could be clear in their communications. They could insist on speaking truth.

Judging by the pastors and organizational leaders I know first-hand, I am convinced the orphan spirit is running rampant in corner offices and senior pastor studies alike. God desires a different reality for us, a life of security, clarity, and care. We owe this level of health to the people we lead. We owe it to ourselves.

5

HOW TO SPOT A SLAVE

Recently a pastor who was visiting the church of a mutual friend walked through that church's brand-new multimillion-dollar facility and was awestruck by the dramatic architecture, the expansive auditorium, and the elaborate decor. Moments later a Twitter update from him appeared on my phone: "If you think *you're* doing something big for God, you should see *this* place!"

I stared at the words on my screen and thought, *Wow. Have those of us in ministry really reduced our mission to who can build the biggest building?*

Contrary to popular opinion—held mostly by spiritual slaves—he who dies with the shiniest stuff really doesn't win. There is nothing inherently wrong with the fineries of this fleeting life, but to define our effectiveness according to them? A fool's game, and nothing more.

Spiritual slaves are "human doings" trapped in the bodies of human beings. They are orphans who are trying to *work their way into God's favor* instead of accepting grace as their way in. But if we have been redeemed by Christ's work, then we have nothing left to prove; eternally and completely, we've already been proven by God.

Spiritual slaves are orphans held captive by the pernicious lie that their worth still hinges on their works.

＊ॐ＊

Max Lucado tells the story of being dropped by his insurance company years ago because of one too many speeding tickets and an inconsequential fender bender that he promises wasn't his fault. One day he received a letter in the mail, informing him to seek coverage elsewhere, and as he reflected on how demoralizing it was to be told he just wasn't good enough according to the company's stringent standards, the spiritual tie-in was too obvious. "Many people fear receiving such a letter," Lucado writes. "Some worry they already have." Lucado then imagines the correspondence, straight from the Pearly Gates Underwriting Division:

> Dear Mrs. Smith,
> I'm writing in response to this morning's request for forgiveness. I'm sorry to inform you that you have reached your quota of sins. Our records show that, since employing our services, you have erred seven times in the area of greed, and your prayer life is substandard when compared to others of like age and circumstance.
> Further review reveals that your understanding of doctrine is in the lower 20th percentile and you have excessive tendencies to gossip. Because of your sins you are a high-risk candidate for heaven. You understand that grace has its limits. Jesus sends his regrets and kindest regards and hopes that you will find some other form of coverage.[3]

This is how it goes for a slave, who constantly lives in fear of not knowing enough, not doing enough, not *ever* measuring up. They're in with God one moment, only to fall out with him the next. Born again, not born again, redeemed, condemned to hell — their eternal security is a tennis match, each lob determined by their moral uprightness that day. Everything with God is temporary, and if they screw up, salvation is lost.

It's bondage, plain and simple. And it's an exhausting way to live.

★☻★

When I was in my twenties, I spent an inordinate amount of energy trying to impress pastors, friends, even God, forgetting entirely that I was already in good graces with him. I worked myself to the brink of burnout and almost lost my marriage as a result. You can surrender to faith or capitulate to works, but you can't simultaneously serve both. And it's not just the individual who is harmed by the snare of spiritual slavery. Invariably, slaves are so committed to their rules that they wind up ostracizing the very people they are called to reach.

A few months ago New Life opened its first Dream Center, which is a free medical clinic for underinsured women living in the communities of Colorado Springs. Before the center opened its doors, I made it clear to our church that the spiritual slaves who happened to be part of our fellowship would not be invited to become partners, volunteers, or staff. I explained that visitors to the Dream Center would most likely be people fighting tough battles in life. They might reek of alcohol. They might have railroad tracks up their arms from drug abuse. They might have rotting teeth, thanks to meth having its damaging way. They might have a posse of kids in tow, each fathered by a different man. They might be pregnant even now and not know the dad's last name.

I could just envision a few slavish volunteers showing up for their shifts and snubbing their noses at these seemingly "subpar" folks.

Instead I chose people in our congregation who love grace and live grace and long to spread it around and invited them to help us serve these women in need. "They need a cup of cold water," I said, "not a lecture about the sinfulness that made them thirsty in the first place." *Grace* is what we're supposed to be about. It's the banner we live under. But for centuries, people inside the church have struggled to get this right.

✂

It is generally held that between the sixth and thirteenth centuries AD, Europe suffered both economic and cultural corrosion following the fall of the Roman Empire. The Dark Ages, they are commonly called, referring not just to the financial status of the continent but also to its status spiritually. Despite the example of grace that Jesus had left for his followers to emulate, many supposed lovers of God had turned to works to keep score of their worth. The church caved to human performance, and spiritual slavery was suddenly in vogue.

Then, in 1517, a young, passionate German monk decided he had had enough. He strolled down to his local church building and nailed on the doors his "Ninety-Five Theses," a now-famous document based on three gems from Ephesians chapter 2: salvation occurs by *grace*, not by works; salvation is a *free gift* from God; and all we have to do to achieve right standing in life is simply *receive*.

Rules were out; relationship was in. A brave man named Martin Luther single-handedly turned the tide.

At the time, copies of the Bible were found almost exclusively in the hands of the wealthy and the clergy, privileged and literate members of society. But now, with the onset of the Reformation, God's Word would be printed in multiple languages and in mass quantity and finally distributed to regular people too. And not a moment too soon. Grace was theirs to seize upon; now they could read about it for themselves.

I think about how radical Luther's proclamations must have seemed to his community and then scan the horizon of our churches today and realize, sadly, we have come full circle. A day rarely goes by when I don't encounter a churchgoing slave face-to-face. They focus solely on who they know, where they have been, what they have accomplished, what they are working on now, all the many rules they are dutifully following, and how long it has been since their last sin.

This is not why Jesus Christ clothed himself in flesh, took the weight of our sins on his shoulders, and willingly walked to the cross. He came and lived and served and died and victoriously rose again so that you and I could know freedom and fellowship and then promote it to everyone we find. He did those things so that you and I could live not as orphans or slaves but as beloved daughters and sons.

I want to spend the rest of my days speaking truth born of a fully convinced heart. God accepts me and radically loves me. He embraces me and calls me his own. Who *he* is and what *he* is up to in my life — these things are worth boasting about.

6

SINNERS SIN

Many moons ago my favorite pastime was dipping snuff. My first experience with chewing tobacco occurred at a family reunion when I was seven years old and one of my uncles handed me a wad. Uncle D was an avid chewer, and I guess he thought it would be fun to teach me how to dip. He used Brown's Mule at the time, the kind of snuff you bite off instead of fingering from a can, and to this day I can recall the sensation of gnawing off a corner of the bitter brown block. But once I had the wad in my mouth that first time, I wasn't at all sure what to do. And so, after tonguing it slowly between my lips and my gums, I swallowed it whole—down the hatch in one gulp.

I vomited all night long, but that didn't dissuade me from getting right back on that horse. Or mule, as the case may be. I rode my beloved Brown's Mule all the way through junior high and into high school, when I promoted myself to Copenhagen, the brand that came in the can that left the indentation on the back pocket of cool people's jeans. My buddies and I had names for the kids who didn't "wear the ring," and none of those names were nice.

My dip-fest continued undeterred until my early twenties, when I was just weeks into my relationship with my then-girlfriend

Pam. Astonishingly, she wasn't interested in dating someone whose bottom lip was always bulging with a fresh, wet chew, but given that her own grandmother also dipped, Pam's frequent ultimatums didn't carry that much weight. Come to think of it, I guess my own grandparents also chewed; growing up, many drinking glasses in our home were just old, thick snuff jars, cleaned out and ready for use.

Shortly after things turned serious between Pam and me, I also got serious about Christ. Within a few days of deciding to pursue his will for my life instead of my own, my decadelong can-a-day habit screeched to a halt. Despite my great fondness for it all those years, there came a day when even the *thought* of snuff made me feel sick. I no longer craved it. I no longer bought it. I no longer chewed it. I no longer spit. In an instant, Christ changed the desires of my heart, and regarding dip, at least, I never looked back.

Furthermore, I became incensed over *other* people's decision to chew. The scent of snuff on someone's breath made me question their intelligence. Didn't they know they were asking for tongue cancer, lip cancer, cheek cancer, gum cancer, throat cancer, tooth loss, and more, with a disgusting habit like that? Plus, only a hick would walk around with that protruded lip and actually believe he looked good.

Interesting, isn't it, how an avid dipper can become anti-dip overnight?

Along the way, I have made an observation about Christ followers: if we're not careful, as soon as we experience victory over a particular habit or sin in our lives, we might become wildly intolerant of that propensity in others. The activity itself could be anything — pornography, misuse of alcohol, gossip, mismanagement of money, or a deep and abiding fondness for that Copenhagen high — but once we find ourselves finally released from its grip, we judge everyone who's still captive.

It's 180 degrees away from the response Christ encourages us to have.

Here's a helpful axiom for the next time you are repulsed by someone's life: Dogs bark, cats meow, and sinners sin.[4] After all, what else is a sinner to do?

The truth is that I *loved* my sin before I surrendered my life to Christ. You probably did too. And if we felt like being honest, you and I would probably also admit that there are *still* sins we struggle to hate. But it's in the midst of the melee that Jesus comes and says, "I am the path to freedom you seek. And I will love you while you're waiting for victory."

My take on Jesus' posture toward the maligned Pharisees in his day is that he was less angered by their rule keeping and more angered by their refusal to let outsiders in. Once you violated the law, you were banned from their fellowship, never to be readmitted again. The woman caught in adultery comes to mind. She had been caught on the fringes of society and wanted desperately to be restored, and the reason why the Pharisees were furious was that Jesus audaciously let her back in.

Among themselves, the Pharisees were a loving, generous, compassionate people. But for people outside that inner circle, the reception was icy cold. When I look at churches today, I see that not much has changed. We say we are kind and caring and focused on freeing people in Jesus' name. But as soon as one from our fellowship falls, we quietly usher him or her out the back door.

May God have mercy on us all.

Dogs bark, cats meow, sinners sin. And Christ followers embrace them still. Wouldn't it be great if that last part were as obvious as the first three? Here is a decent starting point, for you and me both today: When we see a sinner sinning, instead of judging and casting aside, let's commit to taking another tack, to seeing what God might do. Ask a question, encourage a heart, be a friend, meet a need. Despite the very real repulsion we are tempted to feel, let's choose instead to let people in.

7

HOW, NOT WHAT,
I'M DOING

I ran into a friend this week I hadn't seen in quite some time, and after the superficial greetings, he caught my eye, paused, and asked sincerely, "Brady, how are you doing?"

I don't know about you, but typically, when someone asks how I'm doing, I begin to rattle off the week's activities and goings-on: I'm doing this, I'm not doing that, I'm involved here, I'm considering involvement there, and so forth.

But that's not what my friend had asked. He wasn't asking *what* I was doing. What he was asking was *how*.

It was a question that stuck with me awhile. How *am* I doing? Not on the outside: I know how I'm doing there. I've been a Christian a long time and know how to look the part, act the part, dress the part, and talk the part. The externals are fine. But how am I doing on the *inside* — that is what I wanted to know.

✳⚬✳

The next day, during a few quiet moments with God, I sensed him saying, *Remember your friend yesterday? I sent him to ask you that question.*

I can't say I was surprised. For the six months leading up to that brief exchange with my friend, my life had been rather chaotic. I had been uprooted from Dallas and had moved my family to Colorado Springs, and I had accepted a new role in a completely new environment, which upended my relational world. It was joy-filled chaos, but chaos nonetheless. And frankly, I was weary, which I deduced is why God sent the friend my way.

"Father, how *am* I doing?" I asked God, figuring he probably knew the truth.

He didn't answer me directly but instead posed a series of questions himself.

How is your heart?

How are your thoughts?

How are your motives these days?

How are you feeling about your proximity to me?

How has your soul shrunk or grown?

They were questions that spoke not to my activity but to my allegiance—questions of *how*, not of *what*.

+✂+

During his earthly ministry, every time Jesus asked a crowd how they were doing, the Pharisees among them responded by rattling off a report card: "Well, these people over here aren't following the Law. And those folks there are slacking off in six different ways ..."

Time and again Jesus would say, "Hold it, guys. I wasn't asking about behavior. What I'm interested in is the state of your *hearts*."

How. Not what.

Jesus had credibility in these discussions, because Jesus was a "how" kind of guy.

One day, Jesus traveled from Galilee to the Jordan River, where he asked his cousin John to baptize him. We looked at this scene a few chapters ago, but let me draw your attention to one further point: The text says that John stood with Jesus and lowered him into the river, and that as he was raising him out of the water, "heaven was opened, and [Jesus] saw the Spirit of God descending like a dove" (Matt. 3:16). A voice from heaven then said, "This is my Son, whom I love; with him I am well pleased" (v. 17).

Now, this baptism occurred following an eighteen-year period of silence from Jesus Christ. In the Bible, we read about him being born, being a baby, being a young adolescent learning carpentry as a trade — and then *poof.* He disappears. Nothing is recorded about Jesus' life from age twelve to age thirty, when he starts his ministry in full.

But if Jesus' ministry was just *beginning,* how could God already be well pleased? Shouldn't God have saved his praise for *after* all the conversions and healings and raising of people from the dead?

As it turned out, God's timing was just right. True to form, our Father was far more interested in the person than in the performance — *how* his children are doing, not what.

8

NO CONDEMNATION.
REALLY.

When I was a kid, my family lived across the street from another of my uncles and his wife, Willard and Sybil—Uncle Red and Aunt Sybil, to me. Uncle Red was small, short, and feisty, as the fire in his hair implied. Plus, he was the scrappiest fighter I had ever seen.

In our town, if you disrespected a man, you had better be prepared for a punch or two. People in those days defended their honor with their fists, not their words. And certainly not with their prayers. Uncle Red had spent his entire childhood sticking up for his brother—my dad—which made him a hero to my brother and me. We wanted to be just like Red when we grew up, a dream that was only perpetuated by the wild tales he told us.

My uncle wasn't well-off financially, but he had a few prized possessions that he planned to sell one day for a profit or pass down as heirlooms to his kids. One of those treasures was an antique radio, circa 1920, which he kept on a high shelf in the rear of the house.

Uncle Red's radio was encased in ornately carved wood and boasted cloth-covered speakers in front. Even at seven years of age, I understood perfectly well that this particular item was far more than just a box with fabric and knobs. Still, that knowledge didn't stop me, being the punk kid I sometimes was, from destroying my uncle's antique.

My brother and sister and I were always over at Uncle Red's, seeing what fun projects he was up to, taste-testing Aunt Sybil's latest round of baked goods, causing the general mayhem that young kids tend to stir up. One summer afternoon I meandered to the back of the house and found myself standing underneath the shelf where that radio proudly stood. I glanced over my right shoulder, and then over my left. *All clear.* I scrambled up a stepladder and pulled the radio down. And then curious seven-year-old fingers poked giant holes through those speakers' tight cloth.

Later that day, when I was out on the front porch, Uncle Red came storming out of the house with such ferocity that his frame nearly punched a hole through the screen door. "Brady!" he bellowed, making the tiny hairs on the back of my neck stand up. "Brady!" he yelled again, this time right in my face. "What did you *do*? Why did you do it, Brady? WHY DID YOU DO IT? Look at what you did to my mint-condition antique!"

He held up the wooden box, the fabric from its once-perfect speakers now flapping gently in the wind. I had never seen my uncle this angry before, and certainly never at *me*. In that moment, even as a child, I knew that things would never again be the same.

✦⚊✦

It took me many years and many tears to get over the wronging of Uncle Red. And while I would trump that event with far more significant indiscretions throughout my life, that initial disappointment from my beloved uncle was a two-ton brick on my soul. I couldn't believe what I'd done. Even now, I shake my head at my idiocy.

I know I'm not alone in my propensity to look back on my life at all the radios I've poked and feel nothing but sorrow, remorse, and shame. My impetuousness, selfishness, small-mindedness, and greed—how God could see fit to rescue me is beyond me.

And therein lies the rub. Because *I* struggle to forgive a guy like me, I struggle to believe God would do so. Because I can't see past my sinful past, I believe God can't see past it either. Because I feel condemnation toward the man in the mirror, I assume God feels condemnation toward me as well. And maybe without fully intending to, I lock myself in a prison of self-induced guilt and throw away the key.

But this is not what God wants for me. And it's not what he wants for you.

✄

Author and speaker R. T. Kendall wrote an entire book on this subject of forgiving ourselves. In it he lists these ten reasons why we simply must do so:

1. It is precisely what God wants you to do.
2. Satan does not want you to forgive yourself.
3. You will have inner peace and freedom from the bondage of guilt.
4. The degree to which you forgive yourself may directly relate to your usefulness.
5. Totally forgiving yourself will help you love people more.
6. People will like you more when you have forgiven yourself.
7. It will enable you to fulfill all God has in mind for you and thus keep you from being paralyzed by the past.
8. Your own physical health could be at stake.
9. Your mental and emotional health could be at stake.

10. You should forgive yourself because your spiritual state is at stake.[5]

To that last point, Kendall says that when we don't forgive ourselves, we grieve the Holy Spirit. "When the Spirit is grieved ... we are left to ourselves. The result is that we are irritable, have no presence of mind, cannot think clearly, and have little or no insight as to the next step forward. It all comes down to this matter of total [self-]forgiveness."[6]

A good friend of mine can relate to this idea all too well.

Tim was raised by Christ-following parents and was fond of the local church, but when he hit his late teens, he walked away from the faith he had said he loved. Instead of holding down a job and contributing to society in any meaningful way, for months at a time he would disappear to Alaska, working in the fishing industry, blowing all his money on drugs and alcohol. Years went by, and still he frittered his life away, even as his parents faithfully prayed for him to wise up. They trusted God's redemptive power in their son's life, despite their son's having no use for God.

In the fall of 1997, Tim's dad made plans to attend a Promise Keepers event, to be held on the National Mall in Washington, D.C. He invited Tim to attend and, to his surprise, the wayward son said yes. A cross-country flight later, man and son stood with nearly a million other men and listened to speakers such as Max Lucado, James Robison, and Coach Bill McCartney call the crowd to drop their denominational differences and lead the young men of the next generation with intentionality and unity and grace. The dad prayed throughout the entire event that the Holy Spirit would compel his son to get his life back on track. He just knew God would answer his prayer.

What he didn't know was that his son had a far different goal for the day.

Every few hours, Tim excused himself for a bathroom break. And while his dad was there on the Mall praying for Tim's redemption, Tim would be crouched in a portable toilet, getting high on the dope he had brought.

Late that afternoon, Tim told his dad he needed a break from the crowd and that he was going to take a walk. He found a quiet park nearby, and as he was walking down the paved path, the speakers' voices reverberating across the Mall, he experienced a sense of anxiety, fear, and dread on par with nothing he'd ever known. Overwhelmed by darkness and oppression, he began to tremble physically and felt beads of sweat break out across his forehead. His own personal earthquake left as instantaneously as it had arrived, but the sixty seconds of tumult would leave him forever changed. Later he would refer to this moment as his Damascus Road experience.

On his flight home, Tim could not stop thinking about the fear he had experienced there in that park, and he knew he needed to get his life right with God. After walking away from God for nearly fifteen years and living a life of bondage to drugs and alcohol, he began to rediscover his long-lost relationship with the One he had loved as a young teenager.

On a Sunday morning a few months after the Promise Keepers event, Tim was attending a church service with some friends in Washington state. As he quietly sat there during Communion, God took him back to that episode near the Mall when he had experienced such great fear. God then showed him what had happened as he was walking away from the Mall that day.

God silently spoke to him. *Tim, I wanted you to know what it feels like to be outside the umbrella of my protection. Your parents' prayers for you have caused me to keep my hand on you. My desire was for you to stop walking away from me and walk toward me. So for a moment I took my hand of covering away from you so that you would know what it is truly like to walk away from me. And that is when you experienced fear like you never had before.*

Tim finally understood what happened that day in Washington, D.C. Overwhelmed with God's goodness, he fully received the forgiveness offered to him from his heavenly Father.

✢✢✢

It wasn't just the drugs that had fogged Tim's thoughts all those years; what held him back was his refusal to believe that God really does offer a perfectly clean slate. It wasn't what Tim had done or not done that mattered most to God. What counted was that he was now choosing to submit.

That's still all it takes. Moment by moment, we come to God and say, "Show me the me you somehow see." Accepted, approved, embraced, forgiven—if only we would catch this idea.

✢✢✢

When Jesus was facing sure death—an innocent man hanging on a criminal's cross—there were two thieves also being crucified on either side of him. They had been judged and condemned and now were facing the reality of their sentence. One of the thieves looked at Jesus and hurled insults at him. But the other thief, realizing that a sinless man was hanging at his side, said, "Jesus, remember me when you come into your kingdom" (Luke 23:42). In other words, "If you really are who I think you are, and you really can do what I think you can do, then please, if there is any possible way to spare me from the future I am about to experience, I beg you, rescue me."

"Truly I tell you," Jesus replied, "today you will be with me in paradise" (v. 43).

It didn't matter what that thief had done. It didn't matter whom he had harmed. It didn't matter how he had lived, the choices he had made, the number of radio speakers he had impetuously ruined. What mattered was that in this all-important moment he chose to put his faith in Jesus Christ—in earnest and all-out surrender.

This is what arrests the endless loop of awful memories that otherwise plays incessantly in our minds: *"There is now no condemnation for those who are in Christ"* (Rom. 8:2).

We either live life believing we are condemned or we live believing we are forgiven. There is no middle ground here; we are either embracing our past or embracing our future. We can't do both at the same time. It need not take many years or many tears to walk in the freedom we seek. A single moment of surrender and God says, *You are free.*

9

MRS. BRIGHT

When I was a freshman in high school, my English teacher was a crotchety killjoy named Mrs. Bright. She always wore bulky double-knit dresses and a scowl on her face, but the glower was understandable. In those days and in our neck of the woods, most classes were segregated by gender, and having a roomful of hungry teenage boys during the hour just before lunch would have made even Mother Teresa mean.

While school cafeterias never have been known for stellar cuisine, ours was staffed by hefty East Texas women who knew how to fatten up kids. Mashed potatoes and gravy, juicy slices of meat loaf, homemade apple pie — you can't imagine my caloric intake during the first year of high school. The lunchroom happened to be just down the hall from my English class, which meant I could always smell homemade butter rolls rising to perfection, even as Mrs. Bright hassled me about properly conjugating verbs.

Granted, Mrs. Bright had no choice but to be militaristic. She knew that she couldn't afford to smile, relax, or tolerate misbehavior of any kind, because if given even an inch of leeway, my friends and I always took a mile. As a result, on more than a few occasions, I found myself in Mr. Lowry's grip, awaiting a well-deserved paddling.

Mr. Lowry was our school's assistant principal, and he had a special paddle that he would use on disruptive freshman boys. It had a series of holes drilled in it to give the blows a little more force, and about once a week I would see one of my buddies get dragged out into the hallway and then hear three steady swipes—*pow! pow! pow!* You'd think I would have learned from my pals' pain, but you would be giving me far too much credit. Every now and then, Mrs. Bright would spear me with her gaze and point that thick index finger toward the hallway. I knew what that meant.

Eventually, *thankfully*, I was rescued from my plight. Dad's boss, as well as a little divine intervention, saved the day.

A few weeks before I began my sophomore year of high school, my father received a job transfer, which meant my family got to pack our belongings and head to Simsboro, Louisiana. I enrolled in a brand-new school, and my English teacher was a man named Mr. Burt. Perhaps the most creative, energetic, passionate teacher I had ever had, Mr. Burt single-handedly inspired me to welcome grammar as a friend and, later, to work toward a minor in English literature.

Mr. Burt was classically handsome and athletic—the kind of guy every teenage girl swooned over and every teenage boy idolized. He was the spitting image of Tom Selleck, back when Tom Selleck was the coolest of cool. He was also Robin Williams in *Dead Poets Society*, long before the movie came out, and he made studying Shakespeare the most entertaining part of my day.

Looking back, switching from one teacher to another seems so inconsequential—but sometimes a simple shift is all it takes to reinvent a life.

✦⚬✦

Many years after those beloved high school days, I came across a verse of Scripture that spread Turf Builder on my sprouting spiritual life. Galatians 3:23–26 says, "Before the coming of this faith, we were held in custody under the law, locked up until the faith that was to come would be revealed. The law was our guardian until Christ came that we might be justified by faith. Now that this faith has come, we are no longer under a guardian. So in Christ Jesus you are all children of God through faith."

So *that's* what the Law was for, I remember thinking. The Law—God's Law—was a necessary "locking up" in anticipation of freedom later on. It was a way to show us that without some sort of rescue, we would stay locked up forever in our futile attempts to follow the rules, measure up, and make the grade with God.

Before we know God through Christ, we are "in custody" under the Law, in the same way that a child who is orphaned today will be appointed a custodian who will help that child grow into a responsible adult. That custodian has all the rights of a parent. He or she has rights over any assets the child possesses, over the child's training, and over the child's protection, which is exactly the role of the Law in the lives of people who don't yet know Jesus Christ.

If you are not a believer in Christ, then the Law is holding you and keeping you until you surrender your life to him. Day by day, that Law will be an irritating reminder to you that you simply cannot measure up to God's standard by relying on your own wit, wisdom, and strength. Mirroring the method used by Mrs. Bright, the Law intends to bear down on you, put restrictions on you, and remind you that you will *never* measure up. So, yes, it can frustrate you and indict you, but it can also serve to point you to Christ.

This is the reason Jesus came to planet Earth—to fulfill the requirements of the Law for derelicts like you and me. Now that his work is complete, you and I and every other human being alive have a choice to make. We can either insist on trying to keep the Law—spending our days racking up more good deeds for God—or trust in the sacrifice Christ made, and in doing so, get transferred to his love-fueled, life-giving class. Whereas the Law said,

"You will never measure up," Jesus says, "You will fall and you will fail, but my sacrifice will cover your sins. Accept my love and live redeemed. *I* am your teacher now."

Ahhh. Sweet relief. Farewell, Mrs. Bright.

Here's the interesting thing: When I was in Mr. Burt's class, I proved myself far more diligent than I ever did for Mrs. Bright. Rules and regulations served only to oppress me, while freedom compelled me to serve. Satisfying a worthy master is infinitely more exciting than slaving away to placate a master who in the end can never be pleased.

We are freed from spiritual slavery to become bond slaves to the living Christ. In other words, once we embrace our identity as God's daughters and sons, it's our *joy* to adhere to his ways. Sometimes a simple shift is all it takes to reinvent a life.

10

TOO GOOD TO BE TRUE

U m, Brady, you probably want to see this." It was my assistant, Karla, framed by my office doorway, a piece of certified mail in hand.

The letter she held was from an elderly woman on the East Coast, who offered a bit of background on her once severely troubled life. I would come to learn that despite her self-admitted failings as a parent, however, her grown children had come to know Christ. And that once they had experienced God's grace for themselves, they began praying fervently for their mom—for her salvation, for a miracle, for Jesus to somehow intervene.

"One of my neighbors told me about how I could be rescued," her letter continued, "and for some reason, that time it stuck. I gave my life to Jesus Christ and have made a real turnaround."

Immediately on the heels of her conversion, the woman had called her kids to tell them the good news, and as you would expect, celebration broke out. Their prayers were finally answered; their prodigal mother had come home at last. The woman had learned from her believing neighbor that she now needed to find a church, a group of other believers with whom she could worship God and grow in her newfound faith. But it was wintertime in Maryland, and she was worried about getting out in the snow.

Her kids, all of whom attend New Life, hatched a plan. "Mom," they said, "until things thaw out up there, you can log on to our church's website and watch our Sunday morning service live." They pointed her toward the right address and buttons, and the following Sunday she joined our fellowship from the comfort of her warm home.

"I watch you online now every week," she continued. "And I just wanted to say thank you for being my online pastor."

In addition to the letter, the envelope contained four gold coins, each weighing one ounce. Current market value: six thousand dollars. "In all these decades, I've never once given a dollar to the church," the letter offered by way of explanation, "but I thought I could just as well start today."

Six thousand dollars equaled an *annual* tithe for some people in our congregation; had she really meant to send that much? Did she understand what those coins were worth?[7]

For the sake of context, at this writing, we are in a down economy. What's more, despite significant tightening of the purse strings since I took the post at New Life, our church is still hip-deep in a mound of seemingly immovable debt. Six thousand dollars in our situation can go a very long way in getting more ministry done in more places around the world. I fingered those coins and felt my head shake back and forth as I thought, *Surely this is too good to be true.*

My thoughts then tumbled toward that email hoax that's been circulating for at least a decade now. Prince Abayomi (among others) from Nigeria writes to tell you that his family has recently acquired 12 billion quadrillion dollars from oil reserves, but that his government will not let him take possession of those funds unless they are issued in U.S. dollars. Can he please deposit the 12 billion quadrillion dollars into your official checking account for thirty days' time, he wonders, and then convert those funds to his country's currency, so that the money can be issued back to him?

In exchange for all your trouble, you will be allowed to pocket 10 percent. (Your calculator probably doesn't process billion quadrillions, so I'll go ahead and tell you that you would be keeping a very handsome wad of dough.) And all he needs in order to complete this lucrative transaction is access to your checking account.

Now, this *is* too good to be true.

✂

I have noticed an unfortunate trend among people who have not yet surrendered their lives to Christ, which is that the healthy skepticism that keeps them from submitting their checking account and Social Security numbers to strange princes in Nigeria somehow bleeds over into their views on spiritual matters. They listen to the good news of Christianity's message with a skeptical eyebrow raised the entire time.

"You were born a sinner and have been a sinner, but you can be set free from sin's effects in your life," a go-getter for God says to one not yet convinced. "Jesus put on flesh and came to earth and died so that you might live. And because of his great sacrifice, you can now live with purpose and in abundance all your days. What's more, when you do reach the day when you breathe your last breath, you can know beyond the shadow of a doubt that you're headed for heaven, into an eternal existence with God. There you'll receive a perfect body, and you'll know no more trial or turmoil or grief."

The well-meaning believer takes a breath and checks for understanding on the not-yet-a-believer's face, but he's quickly deflated by what he sees. It's a look that says, "Mm-hmmm. *Suuure.* Sorry, pal, but it all sounds a little too good to be true."

Something in us just shakes our head at the nuances of grace's good news. A sinless Savior lets us get off scot-free? Yeah, right. Seems about as plausible as a perfect stranger sending us six grand in the mail. But then again, some things really *are* true that have seemed far too good.

✦✠✦

Author Anne Lamott once said that "grace in the theological sense is that force that infuses our lives, that keeps letting us off the hook. It is unearned and gratuitous love; the love that goes before, that greets us on the way. It's the help you receive when you have no bright ideas left, when you are empty and desperate and have discovered that your best thinking and most charming charm have failed you; grace is the light or electricity or juice or breeze that takes you from that isolated place and puts you with others who are as startled and embarrassed and eventually grateful as you are to be there."[8]

And Ms. Lamott has it right: "startled and embarrassed and eventually grateful" is fine; it's *disbelieving* that will cripple the soul.

It *is* true that we were stuck in our sin and that we were hopeless and without access to God. It *is* true that because of our depravity, we deserved nothing better than death. It *is* true that Jesus Christ entered our mess and with kindness to spare took our fall. It *is* true that although we once were unmotivated to live clean lives, because of the Holy Spirit's arrival on our scene, we now crave the things of God.

It's true that once you and I were orphans, but then we became God's sons and daughters. And once a child of his, always a child of his; we're stuck with him for the long haul. Thankfully, joyfully, with jubilation filling our hearts, we are stuck with our heavenly Father for the longest of very long hauls.

It is good, and it is true, this news that seems too good to be true.

11

WHO YOU WOULD BE,
IF YOU CHOSE TO LIVE FREE

n late September, 1862, as the United States marched on toward its third year of civil war, President Abraham Lincoln announced what he called the Emancipation Proclamation, which stated that "all persons held as slaves within the rebellious states henceforward shall be free." The proclamation was to take effect on January 1, 1863 — a date that would be incredibly meaningful to the ongoing lineage of those once-slaves. In fact, in our country today, you may notice that African Americans are far more prone to celebrating New Year's Day than to celebrating Christmas; January 1 marks the moment when they knew not just spiritual liberation but also long-awaited physical liberation.

January 1, 1863, dawned, the proclamation was put into effect, and from that moment on, every step toward the Union's victory meant a step toward freedom for every slave. But before those slaves back in the 1800s could appreciate their newfound deliverance, they had to first *believe* that they were free.

In a phenomenon that sociologists would find fascinating, soon after slaves were informed that the highest authority in the land had freed them and that they could leave their masters' plantations without fearing reprisal of any sort, rather than rushing into freedom expectantly, many of those slaves stayed put. No matter what people told them, they just couldn't believe it was true. Government officials would come knocking on their doors, saying, "Listen, this is no lie. As of this moment, you're no longer obligated to stay here. Get your belongings, leave this property, and get busy living *free*." But still, they dug in their heels, insisting on remaining slaves.

In the slaves' defense, slavery was all they knew. They had grown up as slaves. Their parents had been slaves. Their grandparents had been slaves. Servitude was the only life they had had. What would it be like to live free? Oppression wasn't exactly desirable, but at least it was *known*. They knew what was expected. They knew how to behave and how to follow the rules. They weren't at all sure they knew how to thrive in liberation's landscape, or what would become of them if they failed.

And so they stayed. In captivity. In subjugation. Enslaved.

Sadly, many Christ followers do the very same thing.

✻

Galatians 4 offers a striking image of the person who surrenders to Christ. It says that people who believe in Jesus Christ move from being "under the law" to receiving "adoption to sonship." It continues, "Because you are his sons, God sent the Spirit of his Son into our hearts, the Spirit who calls out, 'Abba, Father.' So you are no longer a slave, but God's child; and since you are his child, God has made you also an heir" (vv. 5–7).

I meet people far too often who think I'm oversimplifying when I talk in these terms. "You're free!" I say to believers who just can't seem to grasp God's grace. "You're no longer a slave in any facet of life. Your Father has

set

you

free.

And still they look at me as if I'm a lunatic. They just can't see fit to *believe*.

"But I still wrestle with the same stuff I've always wrestled with," they protest. "I'll never get freed from this sin."

They tell me that their parents struggled with sin as well, and their grandparents even before them. "We are all just slaves, Pastor Brady," they say. "But at least we have a place to belong."

My spirit screams, *Nooo!* every time. God never intended for us to find comfort in our bondage. He allows bondage only to show himself worthy as the One who sets us free. "Listen," I tell them, "the highest authority in the universe has declared that he wants you to be free. Gather up your belongings, leave this property, and get busy living free."

Jesus came to planet Earth more than two thousand years ago to secure for us pure freedom, to set us free from slavery's yoke. He knew it wouldn't be an easy sell; remember God's own chosen people, the Israelites? It took them forty years to sort out in their minds and hearts that they never had to return to Egypt. Their days of slavery were over; they could now live as daughters and sons. But *forty* years? *Really?* Surely we have more savvy than that.

The reality is that God does not send slaves to the Promised Land. That place is reserved for daughters and sons. We can know Promised Land living only after we get our identity straight. He has abundance and richness and life that is *truly* life in store for us, if only we will learn to live free. I know that even tragic realities feel familiar and safe, but the worst possible thing a slave can do is to determine in his heart to stay put.

12

COMING TO OUR SENSES

Before Pam and I became parents, Saturdays were football days—LSU football, to be exact. Inevitably, that otherwise-relaxing day is now stuffed full with soccer practices, tae kwon do matches, birthday parties, and more. I love it—really, I do. What I don't love is missing live football. Sure, I record the game each weekend, but more times than not, while running around town, I'll bump into a New Lifer who knows of my allegiance to the team, and in their exuberance they'll say, "Hey! Congrats on your Tigers!"

It's not that this keeps me from watching the recorded game later, you understand. It's just that I watch it then with different eyes. Stories read a little differently when you know how they end.

The most powerful parable in all of Scripture, in my view, is that of the prodigal son. You likely know the ending to this one, given its prevalence still today: A loving dad and his grateful son are hanging out on the front porch of their home, their bellies stuffed from the fattened-calf barbecue, their bodies exhausted from all the singing and dancing. The son pulls his new robe tight against the night chill and nods approval at his new shoes, courtesy of his dad. "It's good to have you back, Son," the older man says with a glimmer in his eye, to which the younger man replies, "I never knew that the life I longed for was waiting for me right here at home."

I love that scene. I love the image of a son finally *living* as a son. But it's important to keep in mind that this scene could never have happened without another scene unfolding first. Before the son could receive his father's unconditional love, he had to embrace the idea that "unconditional" meant he had *absolutely nothing to prove*.

✦❈✦

As the story goes, after the son demanded his inheritance from his father, fled his homeland for a foreign country, and squandered his wealth, he admitted to his dad, "I have sinned against heaven and against you. I am no longer worthy to be called your son" (Luke 15:21).

It was classic slave-talk. The son was erroneously equating his worth to his father with his performance instead of his position. Which ought to make sense to us, since we also tend to struggle to believe that anything in this life is unconditional. With doubting hearts, we work to prove ourselves in hopes that we will garner attention from people we love.

We try to prove to demanding parents that we are responsible, diligent kids. We try to prove to successful siblings that *we are* the favored one. We try to prove to a God we believe is mad at us that we're pretty good people in the end. We try to prove to our own faithless hearts that we'll do better—really, we will—next time.

Sure, there is a place for productivity, for glorifying God with hard work (see chapter 23 for more). But what the son had to catch before he could really live as "son" was that his father's love wasn't based on good deeds.

Thankfully, he did catch it—again, we know how this story ends. But he couldn't have done so unless he had come to yet another realization first. In a still earlier scene, here is what went down.

✦✕✦

Just before the son admitted his wrongdoing to his father, the text says, the older man "ran to his son, threw his arms around him and kissed him" (v. 20). Yes, the son would go on to ask for forgiveness from his father. But before the son said a word, the father began running toward him. The son *belonged* here, in his father's house. Truly, he had nothing to prove.

Pastor Jeff Drott was on staff with me at New Life for three years before he and his family moved back to Texas, where he reentered the marketplace to be a pastor to businessmen. Prior to the two of us serving in Colorado, we had ministered together in the Dallas–Fort Worth area, and in addition to our work lives intersecting, the Drott family lived right across the street. His daughters were our babysitters when our kids were very young, our wives were each other's confidants, and our families often vacationed together when summer rolled around. It takes a long time to make an old friend, and I'm lucky that Jeff is an old friend of mine.

If you were to point to a picture of Jeff Drott and ask my son or my daughter who that is, they would both say, "Uncle Jeff." Clearly, Jeff is not a member of our family, but somewhere along the way the Boyds invited him in. Whether he likes it or not, he *belongs* to us—our home will always be his home. Uncle Jeff is more than just known to us; positionally, he's one of our own. He doesn't have to strive or strain for a place to belong, as long as the Boyds are around.

This is what the prodigal son was reminded of as he finally reached home. *I am loved and adored and accepted here! Here is where I actually* belong.

But he couldn't come to that conclusion until another truth penetrated his soul. Let's back up further still.

✦✕✦

Earlier, in Luke 15:20, we read this: "While he was still a long way off, his father saw him and was filled with compassion for him."

I get the feeling from this single line of Scripture that the dad had been eager for his return. Can't you picture that father as he paced the length of the porch, one eye constantly trained on the road leading home? "If I know my boy, he'll be back any minute," the father muttered. "I just *know* my son will come home."

Who knows how long that anxious man waited before he took in the incredible sight. "Wait. Is that what I think it is? Well, would you look at that! Here comes my long-lost boy!"

His persistence finally paid off as he ran to embrace his son.

This prodigal was known by a loving father; he was seen and respected and prized. But he never would have experienced the gift of such a welcome if he hadn't done another thing first.

Before he could be reminded that he was known and loved and that he always had a place to belong, before he could realize that in his father's embrace he had absolutely nothing to prove, before he could rest in the company of his generous dad, enjoying the byproducts of being at home — before all these, he first had to *come to his senses*. And that's where our story begins.

✦※✦

In Luke 15:17, we find the prodigal son destitute, depressed, and alone. He's thinking about how his father has hired help who are faring better than him, and so he hatches a plan to return to his home and beg his father to at least let him serve as a slave. He would receive much more than this in the end, of course. He would receive acceptance and celebration and love. But he never would have discovered those things had he not taken that critical first step. "When he came to his senses," the text says — only then did life begin.

It was true for the now-famous prodigal, and it remains true for you and me too. Whenever we discover that we're a long way off, we can choose to come to our senses right then. At any moment of any day, regardless of where we are in the world, we can arrest our foolish behavior with one subtle nod toward home. When we are unkind to our spouse or short-tempered with our kid or gossipy in the presence of a friend, we can come to our senses in that moment and step into our Father's ready embrace.

When we are greedy or stingy or wasteful or vain, when we are selfish or prideful or rude, when we lose touch with how blessed we really are, even then we can turn toward God. No matter where we've been or what we've done, our Father's embrace stays sure. He knows well what we are sometimes slow to discern — that real life is found only here at home.

13

A SON WHO
KNOWS HE'S A SON

The times when my wife, Pam, and I brought our two adopted kids home from the hospital rank among my sweetest memories. When my son's birth mother handed Abram to me, I experienced more emotion than I had ever known. It was true again when Callie was born — more tears, more joy, more gratitude toward God.

During the kids' younger years, Pam and I decided not to tell Abram and Callie that they were adopted. Certainly we would disclose the information at some point, but we wanted to be sure the timing was right. When the interview process for the senior pastor role at New Life began to heat up in the summer of 2007, however, the media somehow found out that Pam and I were not Abram and Callie's biological parents. So soon after I accepted the position, we decided we had better come clean with our kids so they didn't learn of their background in that week's Sunday paper.

We had just relocated to Colorado Springs and were in a small rental house at the time. After dinner one night, the four of us crowded around our wooden kitchen table, I looked into my children's expectant eyes, and I said, "Mom and I have a great story to tell you two ..."

Abram and Callie were eight and six at the time, respectively, and I wondered how the revelation would hit them. The truth of the matter was that our kids had been orphans; while their birth moms had wanted to keep them, they knew they lacked the resources to give the children the lives they deserved. Would Abram and Callie feel as though they had been unloved and abandoned, or, because of their subsequent adoptions, would they instead consider themselves handpicked? Regardless of how seamless an adoption process goes, many adopted kids learn of their history and can't help but think, *The woman who birthed me didn't want me. Somehow this must be my fault.*

In Abram's situation, his biological mother was a single mom of three when she found herself pregnant with him — a challenging situation, to say the least. Her decision to place Abram for adoption had nothing to do with him, as he had done nothing wrong. But would he choose to see things that way?

Thankfully, after I finished explaining how Pam and I had crossed paths with each of the kids' birth moms and how we had loved Abram and Callie since the day they were born, I was surprised by how few questions they had, by how easily the news went down. As months went by, a question or two would crop up every now and then, but for the most part the kids accepted the fact that they were as much a part of the Boyd family as if Pam and I had conceived them ourselves.

Fast-forward to several months ago, when I was reading to Abram one night before bed. We finished a short passage of Scripture and talked about the best parts of the day; then, before I left his room, I put my hand on his chest and prayed protection and blessing over my son.

As I made my way toward Abram's bedroom door and reached up to turn off the light, I heard a sleepy voice from the other side of the room. "Dad?"

I glanced back at him. "Yeah, buddy?"

"Thanks, Dad," he said. "For adopting me."

"Well, you're welcome, Abram," I said quietly. Taking a step toward him, I asked, "But why did you bring that up?"

Still lying flat on his back, his hands resting on his chest, Abram said, "Well, I just realized that if you hadn't adopted me all those years ago, you and I wouldn't be buddies."

Staring at my boy with the kind of pride that makes a man burst, I said, "Abram, I'm really glad you're my buddy. We'll *always* be buddies, you know?"

Abram nodded. Smiled. Flipped over and faced the wall. I turned to leave, flicking off the light as I went. And after I closed the door behind me, I stood in the hallway for several minutes, sweeping away renegade tears.

In a moment of prayer, I asked God if there was something going on in Abram's heart that I needed to know about, maybe some kind of insecurity surfacing in him, some unrest regarding his adoption. For a few seconds I sensed nothing in reply. But then came a divine reassurance, slowly, silently, clear as could be. *Abram is perfectly fine, Brady. That reminder was for you.*

As I stood at the top of the staircase after saying good night to Abram, I thought about God's goodness in my life. He voluntarily adopted me, not because of my goodness but because of his. I had been chosen, accepted, adopted, loved, purposed, celebrated, embraced. That is the truth Abram resurrected in me on the night when he simply said thanks. And now I could know life as it was meant to be lived.

PART TWO

LIVING WELL-LOVED

Acceptance, approval, adoration, lavish
 accommodation — the
 accoutrements of the place we've longed for.
Everyday life at home.
We rest in grace and walk in his ways.
We live as daughters and sons.
We've belonged since the beginning.
At last we believe it's true.

14

THE PRAYER OF
A RECOVERING SLAVE

The invitation came from a young pastor out east who wondered if I would meet with him—on his home turf—to discuss how a run-ragged pastor possibly finds rest. He had heard a few talks I had given on the subject of surviving burnout, and he hoped that commiserating with one who had been there, done that, and lived to tell about it would save him from flaming out himself.

Our arrangement included my speaking at his church's Wednesday night service after spending the better part of the day meeting in his office to sort out his ministry dilemma. Following the evening service, which went well, the pastor agreed to drive me the forty-five minutes back to my hotel. It had been a productive day, but I had a final lingering question. "Tell me," I said, "when you pray, what is the one thing you always pray for?"

The pastor's eyes lit up as he turned toward me. "Oh, that's easy," he said. "Every time I pray—and I mean *every* time—I say, 'God, please use me today! Just use me, please. My life is yours; use it for good today.'"

He went on this way for a few minutes, describing the substance and style of his usual prayers, and as I listened to him there in the dark of the pickup's cab, I thought, *Ah. Prayers from the heart of a slave.*

I probed a little deeper into his conversations with God and then said, "I want to go back to what you mentioned earlier, about the way you typically pray." I explained that his response struck me as a slave's prayer, the prayer of someone desperate to earn the approval and favor of God. No wonder he was exhausted. He was *working* his way toward God.

His litany of follow-up questions told me he was interested in knowing more.

The thing I told him is what I tell myself on countless occasions. I am a recovering slave who also struggles to rest in God's free gift of grace, and I need this message of freedom as much as anyone I know. Clearly, it is fine to be invited into God's purposes in this world and make yourself available to him. But begging him daily to "use you" is not the language of a son. I am reminded of the character Donkey in the animated Shrek movie trilogy. During the looped screen that runs behind the menu on the DVD version, Donkey is jumping as high as possible to be seen over the other characters gathered in front of the affable ogre. Each time he bounds upward, he yells, "Pick me! Pick me! Pick me!" It's a cute add-in for a kids' movie, but a little pitiful as an approach for coming into the presence of an accepting and loving God.

As his children, we can come before our Father confidently, gratefully, and expectantly, eager to involve ourselves in his ongoing work. Rather than pleading for God's attention, we can relax in his ever-present care.

The more this pastor and I talked, the more I realized where his slave spirit originated. Growing up, he never felt he measured up to his alcoholic father's expectations. He could never hold his dad's attention and never believed he was loved simply for who he was. Even as the young boy became a mature man, that bondage persisted. He had built a life on subtly begging his friends, his

THE PRAYER OF A RECOVERING SLAVE

family, and even his God to find him valuable, worthy, good. But the wearying nature of that approach was destroying him from the inside out. Nothing worth having is begged for; it is always simply received.

Following that quick trip, I reflected on what distinguishes the prayers of daughters and sons from those of orphans and slaves. I was reading Eugene Peterson's memoir, *The Pastor*, and I came across his definition of "pastor" as one whose primary task is to "pay attention and call attention to what God is doing."[9] This is true not only for pastors but also for every daughter, every son. Our prayers are opportunities to discover where God is working and how we can join in. Rather than the focus being on us — Pick me! Pick me! Pick me! — the focus unyieldingly fixes on him.

What are you up to here, Father?
What are you after in this situation?
Where are you working in my corner of the world?
And how can I cooperate with you?

To be freed from slave spirit prayers, I'm learning, is to begin to rest in God's grace.

15

LONE COWGIRL
AT A PRINCESS PARTY

For as long as I can remember, my daughter, Callie, has been such a devoted tomboy that she perceives being asked to wear a dress as punishment. Once, Callie—then age five—came downstairs one afternoon wearing a frilly dress. "You look beautiful!" I raved as she reached the bottom step.

Her curly hair was pinned up like a movie star's, with a regal-looking tiara positioned atop her head—and a scowl was firmly planted on her face.

"What's wrong, Callie?" I asked, as any dense dad would. She had been invited to a friend's birthday party—a princess-themed event—and all of the girls were supposed to wear frilly dresses. I thought my daughter looked great, but obviously I had missed the point.

"It's making me *iiitch*," Callie whined, grimacing more severely. "I don't *waaant* to wear this ..."

"Oh, Callie, you look fine. Now go on to the party. You'll have a blast!"

Thankfully, just as I wrapped up my "encouragement," my better half stepped in. Out of the corner of her mouth, Pam whispered to me, "She really doesn't want to be dressed this way."

Approaching Callie, she said, "Honey, you don't want to be a princess, do you?"

With arms firmly crossed, Callie said, "No!"

It goes down as the best picture of Callie's youth thus far: At that princess-themed party, a photograph was taken of all the guests surrounding the birthday girl, and planted in the middle of a dozen or so frilly dresses is little Callie, surer than sure about who she is, decked out in a pink cowgirl vest, pink chaps over her most comfortable blue jeans, pink boots, and a bright pink Western hat. Her eyes are dancing and her smile is wide. A princess, she is not.

✦᭡✦

That otherwise-inconsequential episode in my daughter's life has stuck with me all these years for one reason: Christ followers too often neglect to live from our God-given identity as sons and daughters and instead settle for playing dress-up. "It is the fear of other people's judgment that prevents us from being ourselves, from showing ourselves as we really are, from showing our tastes, our desires, our convictions, from developing ourselves and from expanding freely according to our own nature," says author Paul Tournier. "It is the fear of other people's judgment that makes us sterile, and prevents our bearing all the fruits that we are called to bear."[10]

When we surrender our lives to Jesus Christ, we become children of the King, immediately eligible for eternity with God in heaven and for abundance here on earth. But more than half of the Christians I come across are living below God's potential for them. They exist in bondage to a flawed self-concept instead of seizing the freedom that is theirs.

A lot of attention has been paid in recent years to the topic of self-esteem, which is what you believe to be true about yourself. It's a far different concept from your identity, which is what is *actually* true of you. The truth about who you are—about every

Christian—is that you have been set free by the cross of Christ, you have been freed to become a child of God. My point is this: Freedom is not about what we have been set free from. Freedom is about what we have been set free to *become*. And who we can become is a son, a daughter, of the King.

If I bought the message so many churches unwittingly broadcast today, I would come away thinking that Jesus Christ came to earth and died a horrific death on a cross for the sole purpose of behavior modification. A little straightening out here, a little acting better there—"moralism," it's commonly called. But Jesus didn't come to correct our behavior; he came to correct our *identity*. I'm all for sinning less; it's just not the reason why Christ came.

God's desire is that you and I would embrace our identity in him. He wants us to reject the role of orphan and slave and opt for the role of daughter or son—and then, once in the family, to allow him to fulfill his purposes for us. We all have different callings. When each of us does our part, God's family is unified and functions well. Not everyone needs to be a princess. We need some decent cowfolk in the mix.

The apostle Paul communicated this truth by using the metaphor of a body (1 Cor. 12). In this body, some of us are called to be the arms, some the legs, some the rib cage, some the big toe. I often tell our congregation at New Life, "Just imagine if all ten thousand of us were fulfilling exactly the role God is asking us to fulfill. Imagine the effect of a body that strong! Imagine if we all were breathing in as one, breathing out as one, loving as one, serving as one, pointing people toward faith in Christ as one. Just *imagine* the impact we'd have."

Our city of Colorado Springs needs that type of strength. It needs thousands of Christ followers who are so secure in the knowledge of who they are—and of *whose* they are—that they leap at the opportunity to be the hands and feet of Christ.

So does the city where you live.

Callie is eleven now, and a few days ago I showed her the picture from that princess party. "Callie," I asked, "doesn't it bother you that you're the only girl not wearing a frilly dress?" To which my confident cowgirl replied, "Nope."

I want to be just like her when I grow up. Most likely, so do you. The first step toward that noble goal is simply acknowledging that God did not mess up when he made you. You are not an accidental invention or the result of some random cosmic collision. You were custom-made by the hand of God even before you took up space in your mother's womb, according to Psalm 139. Once you surrender your life to Christ, you become a carrier of the very Spirit of God. And God doesn't place his Spirit inside mistakes.

You are intentionally designed and terrifically loved, regardless of your tastes, your desires, your convictions, your nature. It's your *you-ness* that God deeply loves. And it's your you-ness that he wants in his home.

16

LESSONS FROM
BACKWOODS TREE LIMBS

When I was a kid, my dad would take my brother, Dave, and me duck hunting nearly every Friday or Saturday afternoon in the winter. Like every other eight-year-old boy in northwest Louisiana, I possessed my own single-shot shotgun and had already racked up several years of exhilarating (albeit fruitless) hunting experience.

Each weekend, Dad would say the word, and Dave and I would scramble to get into our gear, grab our guns, and pile into the pickup truck, ready to go. We would head out to Pace Bottom, which comprises hundreds of acres of oak-tree-dotted swampland bisected by the Sabine River. My dad would remind my brother and me about gun safety, position us underneath separate trees, and then head off to make a blind for himself. We three then would wait silently for a duck to fly toward the marshy water, and as soon as one descended into view — *pow!* — one of us Boyds would take aim and fire. Given the number of hours I spent beneath a tree with a loaded gun tucked under my arm, you'd think I would have bagged dozens of ducks. No such luck. I never got a single one. But of course that wasn't the point. *Adventure* was why my brother and I were there. That, and being with Dad.

In our part of town, there was a rule that you could not hunt after sunset. But my dad, figuring it was often light long after the sun had officially set, always broke the rule. Inevitably, determined to eke out every moment from our beloved duck hunt, we three would hang around until the sun's conclusive wink before traipsing the mile or two back to the truck. By then we would find ourselves shrouded in night's blackest black. My dad was always in the lead, a thick, square Rayovac flashlight pointed at his feet, and Dave and I were made to stay right on Dad's tail, guns unloaded and pointed at the ground, until we reached the truck. Which was fine by us, since otherwise we couldn't see six inches in front of our faces.

My dad had grown up hunting Pace Bottom and knew the area well, but given its vastness, it was easy to get lost. On more occasions than I can count, he would be walking briskly even as he tried to make out which route led back to our truck, one arm clutching his shotgun and the free arm rather absentmindedly sweeping low-slung tree limbs out of his way. Those cold, hard limbs would snap back just as Dave and I approached, and — *whap!* — we'd get nailed in the face every time. To this day, I wonder why all three of us didn't have flashlights. Admittedly, my family was not well-off. But three flashlights? How much could that have set us back? As it turned out, Dave and I would wind up with welts across our face and chest. "What *happened* to you boys?" Mom would predictably ask upon our return home.

Tree limbs, Mom. Again.

On occasion, Dad would take Dave and me on a morning hunt, and that post-hunt walk back to the truck was *immensely* more enjoyable. With the dirt path under our feet still bathed in bright sunlight, my brother and I could see for ourselves where to tread. No snapping tree limbs. No painful welts. No probing questions from Mom. Lesson learned: the trip is always better taken in the light.

✄

I grew up in a pretty legalistic church environment, and what I discovered upon becoming an adult is that for much of my life I had followed a set of rules and deeply ingrained convictions that were nowhere to be found in the pages of Scripture. The customs and traditions I'd been taught weren't inherently bad—in fact, morally, they were quite good. It's just that they didn't show up in God's Word.

In other words, I needed to read the Bible for myself. The only way for me to know what God expected of me was to read the Scriptures on my own and then interpret them aptly, honestly, and rigorously. God's Word is what provides divine guidance. God's Word is what serves as life's map. God's Word is what throws much-needed light on the path when you need your own Rayovac.

I stood before our congregation on a Sunday morning recently, and partway through my talk I asked two questions. First, "How many of you have made a bad decision in the past twelve months?" A few self-righteous folks sat there motionless, but the rest of us quickly raised our hands. Then, my second question: "How many of you would like to know how to make nothing but good decisions in the year ahead?" Even the self-righteous ones wanted in on that. As I told them, if we want to make nothing but good decisions in our finances, in our friendships, in our marriages, in our parenting, in our occupations, in our health—in *every* aspect of life—we need only look to God's Word. Most people believe that Psalm 119 was written by David, as he was reflecting on God's written law. Here is what the psalmist says:

Oh, how I love your law!
    I meditate on it all day long.
Your commands are always with me
    and make me wiser than my enemies.
I have more insight than all my teachers,
    for I meditate on your statutes.

I have more understanding than the elders,
    for I obey your precepts.
I have kept my feet from every evil path
    so that I might obey your word.
I have not departed from your laws,
    for you yourself have taught me.
How sweet are your words to my taste,
    sweeter than honey to my mouth!
I gain understanding from your precepts;
    therefore I hate every wrong path.

Your word is a lamp for my feet,
    a light on my path.
I have taken an oath and confirmed it,
    that I will follow your righteous laws.
— PSALM 119:97–106

We can be wiser than those who oppose us. We can be more insightful than those who have taught us. We can be more understanding than people twice our age. And we can have God's best path illuminated for us, at every fork in the road. A lamp for our feet and light on our path—I defy you to find anything in life more useful and beneficial than that.

✦✧✦

Most nights, I read Scripture to my kids as I'm putting them to bed. We talk about stories in the Bible and about the noble character traits we wish we also possessed. Often I will lay my hands on Abram and Callie afterward and pray over them. "Lord, please let your Word be a lamp for my kids' feet," I'll say. "Please be a light for their path."

Pam and I have only about ten more years during which we get to serve as our kids' primary influence, and then they will be

entering college and adulthood and will make life-altering decisions on their own. That's why I speak that verse over them so pas-
sionately. They won't always have Mom and Dad around to help
them sort out right from wrong. But God will never leave them,
and his Word will never return void. I want Abram and Callie to
fall in love with God's Word in the same way the psalmist did: to
him, God's insights were sweeter than honey. That's what I crave
for my kids and for Pam and me. It's also what I want for you.

If you've been wandering around absentmindedly in darkness,
God has a word for you: *It's time to turn on the light.* You won't acci-
dentally end up on God's perfect path for your life; you've got to
be directed to the steps he'd have you take. If you ignore his guidance and wisdom and plan, you will stumble through your days,
acquiring unnecessary welts at every turn. But if you meditate on
his Word as the psalmist did and ask for his help, the way will be
made clear.

Whatever has you knotted up these days, God's Word can
untangle it. Financial struggle tying you up? Ask God to point you
to the verses you need to be reminded of. Relational stress keeping
you awake at night? Pray for insight and guidance, and then carefully read what God asks you to read. Parenting woes turning your
hair gray before its time? Before you email your friends, call your
family counselor, reread your beloved how-to-fix-your-kid books,
or spend yet another night bemoaning to your spouse your sorry
state, try *turning on the light* instead. Pray, "God, what tools do I
need to be the right kind of parent for my child right now? What
dose of insight do I lack? What ounce of wisdom will help me
through this hour? Please direct me to the Scriptures that can be
my lifeline today." If you don't sense any specific direction, search
the Web for Bible verses on what's on your mind, for starters. Let
the words you find spur you to deeper study. Trust God's Word to
guide you; his instruction is just what you need.

That church I grew up in—the one that said bowling, dancing, and playing cards were evils on par with committing murder, adultery, and theft—taught me to believe that anything fun was sin and anything not fun was of God. But now I know better. I have experienced for myself that when I follow the path God encourages me to tread, life explodes with adventure and joy. I only thought I knew what fun was, back when I was calling the shots for myself. The truth is, the trip is *always* better when it's taken in the light.

17

MONDAY-MORNING CONFESSIONS FROM A SUNDAY-LOVING PASTOR

Dear God,

It's Monday morning following Easter Sunday, but I suppose you are already aware of that. I hope you were pleased with what happened at church yesterday. By the way, thanks for being there. Church is always better when the One we have gathered to encounter shows up. I hope you were honored by our worship and given full permission to move in our midst.

I love Sundays, and yesterday was no exception. I never tire of sensing your presence. To watch your Spirit move in people's hearts here these days, engaging them, transforming them, establishing in them deeper faith and peace, feels like something out of Acts 2. What a gift to see new life emerge. I never grow weary of watching you work: more than one hundred new believers were baptized; scores of others surrendered to Christ.

So, yes, how I do love Sundays; it's Mondays I wish I could skip.

Monday is when my body pulses with the ache of energy expended all weekend long. Monday is when my mind feels like mashed potatoes—a pile of heavy, sticky goo. Monday is also when post-service criticism wiggles its way into my soul. Will I ever get better at receiving "helpful corrections" mere seconds after I come down from the stage? Don't the criticizers know how drained and vulnerable I am after pouring my heart out up there? How I wish they would wait a day or a week before slashing the details to shreds.

Ah, Monday. Satan's playground, if I'm not careful. The day of each week when I feel my limitations most. Exhaustion, frustration, depletion, despair—it's amazing how the highest high of the week gives way to the lowest low.

Still, I thank you on this, a Monday, admittedly my least favorite day. I thank you for being my strength when I'm tanking and for accomplishing kingdom objectives through such an imperfect, sometimes-petty man. I recognize the impossibly high stakes every time I speak—eternal life, eternal death, the choice that looms. And I tell you with fresh enthusiasm that I take seriously this role that I have. I am grateful to pastor New Life. I am humbled by your calling on my life.

Keep me focused on the things that matter, Father, and help me overcome my carnal ways. On this day when I am more in touch with my desperate need for you than on any other day of the week, please cover me with your sufficiency and grace. Please show me how to live Monday as your son.

Thanks for the always-open ear.

Forever your son,

Brady

18

DISAPPOINTED WITH GOD

To Pam and me, moving from Shreveport, Louisiana, to Amarillo, Texas, was the equivalent of trudging to the ends of the earth. It was the 1990s, we had been married only a few years, and we had just waved goodbye to every family member and friend we had. A year into our Texas stint, we both were incredibly lonely, so we asked God to take us back home. "Would you open the door to a job opportunity in north Louisiana?" we'd beg him, hoping desperately he would pull through for us. One day we thought he had.

I had had a random meeting with a man in town, who introduced me to a guy who owned several television stations. That station owner and I connected, and out of the blue he offered me a job running one of his stations—in north Louisiana, of all places. I was thirty years old with a dusty journalism degree, thinking I had just caught the world by the tail.

When he called to formalize his offer, I was sitting at a tiny table in our tiny kitchen of the tiny house we owned, and as I scribbled each detail on my yellow legal pad, Pam looked over my shoulder and whispered, "Wow!" I nearly choked when the guy spouted off the salary, which represented more money than I had ever made in my life. He also wanted to pick up expenses for our move and for an apartment to rent until we could settle into a house of our own.

I hung up the phone, turned to my wife, and said, "Honey, we're going *home*."

✄

Just after the station owner had laid out the entire package, I'd told him that I was a Christ follower and that I wanted to pray about it before I said yes. But he and I both believed that to be a formality; only a fool would say no to the offer. Still, I said, "Give me a day to think things through; I'll call tomorrow with my final word."

Wanting at least to offer up a courtesy prayer to God, I told Pam I was going for a walk. It's not that I didn't want God's input on the decision; it's just that his fingerprints were so obviously all over the opportunity that I felt it was a bit ridiculous to ask him, "So, Father, what do you think?"

I descended the handful of steps leading from our front porch to the sidewalk, elated over the phone call I'd just had, and before I could even say word one of my prayer, I sensed God say clearly, *No*.

Stopping in my tracks, I looked up at the night sky and said, "Huh? God, was that you?"

Again: *No*.

If it had been audible, it would have been yelled. It was that definitive and clear and strong.

"But God," I said, "I haven't even asked you anything yet."

A third time: *No*. Then, *I am well aware of the question, Brady, and I'm telling you, the answer is no.*

My mind swirled in confusion. "But we've been begging to move back to Louisiana. Isn't this the answer to all of those prayers?"

No. No. No.

"But God, surely you heard that guy's offer. How am I supposed to say—"

The. Answer. Still. Is. No.

I felt as if I was stuck in a bad dream. With head bowed and heart low, I walked back up the stairs, entered the house, and said to Pam, "God said no." In the time it took for me to walk the round trip from our kitchen to the front yard and back again, our hopes and dreams had been dashed.

✦✗✦

If I lined up a hundred people who had followed Christ faithfully across several decades and who had suffered great loss along the way and asked them, "Do you regret your life—the tough stuff you had to walk through?" I guarantee they would all say no, they don't regret it a single bit.

Now, if I also asked them if they cared to repeat those dark nights in the valley, I can promise you, to a person they would again say no. But they would rule that the pain had been worth it for what they learned of themselves and of God.

Blessed is the man, *blessed* is the woman, who does not fall away (Matt. 11:6) even when life gets hard, even when we are disappointed with God. These were the words Jesus had spoken to John the Baptist, via John's disciples, on the heels of his question to Jesus regarding whether he was the real deal they'd been expecting or whether his followers should continue to wait.

Interestingly, John had posed the question from prison, where he had been locked up for preaching in Jesus' name. Imagine you do every single thing God asks you to do, and you get tossed in the slammer as a result. I daresay John was familiar with divine disappointment, which is likely why he posed the question. "Jesus," he asked, "my friend and cousin and Master too—are you the One we've been expecting, or are we still waiting for someone else?" (see Matt. 11:2).

True to form, Jesus didn't answer directly. Nor did he acknowledge that his friend/cousin/follower was locked up in a prison cell. Instead he said to John's messengers, "Go back and tell John what's going on: The blind see, the lame walk, lepers are cleansed, the deaf hear, the dead are raised, the wretched of the earth learn that God is on their side. Is this what you were expecting? Then count yourselves most blessed!" (Matt. 11:4–6 MSG). (Notice that Jesus conveniently left out the part about captives being freed. He didn't want to get John's hopes up, after all.)

This passage schools me every time. What was Jesus saying? Was he intentionally being cruel? It surely would be easy to think so, if you're the one in the prison cell. But we know better. We know more of our great God.

I think Jesus was saying, "Listen, I know you can't see past your chains to appreciate the change going on in the world. But the reasons why I came are being worked out here and now. My Father's bigger purposes are being fulfilled. And even though all you know is disappointment today, you'll be blessed for all your tomorrows when you do not fall away."

Several months after I called the station manager back and told him that while I knew it would make no sense to him, I simply couldn't accept the job, Pam and I met with a woman who had an interesting proposition for us. God was about to answer an even bigger prayer than the prayer about moving home. He was about to give us the son we had dreamed about since our first days as man and wife.

God is working at all times on our behalf in the invisible realms, and he is well aware that all of that invisibility will cause us distress from time to time. The job doesn't pan out. The house doesn't sell. The marriage doesn't last. The runaway doesn't return. The investment doesn't yield viable returns. Circumstances scatter our dreams and wreck our plans. Or so it seems, anyway. We simply cannot see what God sees. We cannot know what he alone knows.

And so we wrestle. We admit disappointment. We engage in earnest dialogue with our God. But in the end, whether resolution is reached or not, we come around to the same vow: "I will not fall away. I trust you, Father. I really do. And while I don't understand what you're doing, I know you are guiding me along righteousness' path. I'm disappointed but not disheartened, Lord. You're still God, and you are good."

19

HEAVEN BREAKING THROUGH

Mother's Day.

For years, there was no more dreaded date on the calendar for Pam and me. She desperately wanted to be a mother, and I desperately wanted to see her in that role. But the children we prayed for and pined for and craved never saw fit to show up. We had spent thousands of dollars we didn't really have to undergo test after disheartening test. Each one told us the same thing: neither of us was physically able to help conceive a child. Perhaps the worst part of that string of procedures was the depressing postgame talks. One doctor or another would sit across from us and say, "I'm sorry, Mr. and Mrs. Boyd, but unless something miraculous happens, being parents is just not in your cards."

Eventually we ran out of money, and it was then that we said, "God, if you want us to have children, the situation is in your hands. We've done everything we can possibly do toward this goal, and still we're a family of two."

We were in our midtwenties at the time, and it seemed that the only thing our married friends had to do was brush past each other, and they would be pregnant the following week. Babies were everywhere we looked — that is, except in our little home. We were dejected, vulnerable, exhausted, and sad, and it was always when we were in this particularly sorry state that Mother's Day had the gall to roll around. Each time, Pam and I would have good intentions of heading to church, but the ache in our hearts kept us away. We would call our moms with greetings of gratitude and love, our upbeat voices cloaking immense grief and pain. We would head for a restaurant and hide out for a few hours and then go to the movies alone.

"Medical impossibility" was the precise phrase one doctor used during one of those agonizing chats, and so Pam and I decided that before we gave up, we would ask God to let heaven break through. In our minds, heaven breaking through in this instance equated to the miraculous healing of both of our bodies. What had been impossible would become possible, and we would praise God the rest of our lives. "Heal us so we can have children," we prayed, "and we'll raise them to love you and fear you and serve you all their days."

It seemed like a reasonable trade to us. And so we prayed it night and day. *We know you're powerful enough to heal us, Father. We trust you want to see us raise kids. We believe you will do this great work for your glory. Please, God, heal us now.*

God's answer to us was no.

Or at least that's what we thought.

Years after our initial prayers, a pastor from our church called and asked if we would be willing to meet with a woman from our fellowship. We knew of the woman but certainly didn't know her well. We hadn't seen her in nearly a year and hadn't kept up with her life, so we were shocked when we walked into the appointed meeting place and saw that she was six months along.

"I feel like God has been whispering to me," she explained, "that you are to be the parents of this child."

The kingdom of heaven tends to break through in ways far different from what we plan or expect.

Two years later another mom approached us, three weeks from her delivery date. Knowing she couldn't provide her baby with the upbringing she wanted to give her, and swayed by her own mother's encouragement to pursue adoption for the child, she single-handedly grew our family from three members to four.

I had always dreamed of having a little redhead with blue eyes, and as I thought about this young mom's auburn hair, her sparkling turquoise eyes, I knew our meeting had been more than a chance encounter. I knew I was watching heaven break through. Earnestly we told her we would pray about our decision, even as our hopes flew sky-high.

Abram and Callie are Boyds today, thanks to heaven's propensity to seep into our lives and prove to us that God is still mightily at work.

Pam and I learned something on the heels of that emotionally and physically draining season. We learned that there is no cheap way to follow Jesus, that intimacy with him will likely continue to require every single thing we have. Clearly, we could grow a bigger church if we had a more positive message than that, but we don't. So we won't. And that is fine by us. A yes to God means a no to ourselves. It means at times humiliation and disillusionment and pain. But I can tell you from firsthand experience what it also means: being swept up in the magnificence of heaven breaking through to the brokenness of this life we lead.

Whatever dreams have been put to death on this path I'm on have been replaced with richer realities still. Whatever price my God should ask me to pay will be worth it in the end.

20

EPIC MESSES

Just after 10:00 a.m. on January 8, 2011, twenty-two-year-old Jared Lee Loughner opened fire on a "Congress on Your Corner" session hosted by third-term United States Representative Gabrielle Giffords in the parking lot of a Safeway grocery store in her home state of Arizona. Representative Giffords sustained a shot to the head at point-blank range, eighteen others were shot—six of them fatally—and a nation found itself once again unnerved. Giffords would live through the experience, but certainly not unchanged.

In the days following the shooting, I thought about Ms. Giffords and about the man who tried to kill her. With one dreadful decision on one otherwise-ordinary day, he made an epic mess of his life.

On some level, I know how he feels. Granted, my sins may not be as consequential as his in the eyes of the law, but they are in the eyes of God. I have made equally devastating decisions along the way, and while they may not have resulted in another person losing his life, they certainly resulted in my hamstringing my own.

And I know I'm not alone.

I've been taking a poll among my Christ-following friends—the ones who have been walking with Jesus for two decades or more. "Even after all this time as a Christian," I ask, "do you find yourself

102

still making a mess of your life?" As I say, the number of knowing nods I get proves that God's job security is firmly intact. Those of us who know him and love him and devote our lives to him still need him with uncanny frequency to show up, mop and bucket in hand. Based on my admittedly anecdotal evidence, either I hang out with some terribly imperfect people or "messy" is what we all are.

I am not encouraging mess-making here; I am not pro-sin. I happen to believe that higher moral conduct is better than immorality, that good behavior is better than bad behavior, and that following the rules is most often better than breaking them just for sport. So I am not giving license for errant living. I am simply acknowledging that wherever human beings live and breathe, messiness exists. But there's another reality that is equally true: God is not put off by our mess.

If I were to sum up the vast beauty of the gospel message in five words, they would be *God willingly enters our mess.* He sees our mess, he feels compassion toward our mess, and he gladly steps right in. That's good news for messy people such as you and me, because God alone possesses the tools required to clean up a situation like ours. To the guy who takes another's life or who sleeps in the wrong person's bed or who seemingly can't speak a single sentence without blaspheming God's name, the response is exactly the same: "I'm not put off by your mess," our Father says, "and I'd love to stay to help clean things up. Open the door to my will and my ways, and I'll be more than happy to come in."

Now, there are two options available to us upon hearing this invitation from God: we either can keep the door of our heart shut tight or we can swing it wide open and welcome him in.

I have heard many definitions of repentance through the years, but the simplest one has to be this: repentance is unbolting the door and throwing it open to God's presence and power and plan. Because when we turn toward that door and reach for the knob, we are necessarily turning away from our mess. The old hymn "Turn

Your Eyes upon Jesus" is more than a catchy tune; it's also sound theology. "Turn your eyes upon Jesus," it says, "look full in his wonderful face. And the things of earth will grow strangely dim, in the light of his glory and grace."[11] We can focus our eyes on Jesus, or we can focus on the messes we've made. But we can't do both simultaneously. Only one gets our attention at a time.

Repentance, I am learning, is admitting I make a lousy god. Worshiping myself always leads to messes, and I am never at peace in a mess.

And so, time after time, sin after sin, I turn. I walk toward that door. I confidently turn the knob, knowing full well who I'll find on the other side. I do this because I want to be a mature follower of Christ. Mature followers make the first move, knowing God won't come in unless asked. That's not to say he's not persistent, though. You can keep the door shut and hope he will wander away, but I guarantee he will stay planted right there. Hours, days, even years later, you will glance at your wife, who is pulling aside the front-window curtain a bit to peek outside, and through the side of your mouth you will whisper, "Still there?" To which she will toss a subtle nod your way, confirming what you already knew.

No, the better bet is simply to repent. We will make a mess, yes. But we can quickly make it right. We can charge toward that door—and away from our mess—and say to God, "Good! I'm glad you're still here." We can throw open the door, welcome him in, and bless his name as he swipes at our stains. "Return to me, and I will return to you," our Father promises in Malachi 3:7. One swift step of repentance, and God rushes our way once more.

Quick to repent. Quick to turn from our mess. Quick to know even baby-step growth. We can either stick with our messes or stick with our Master, the One who makes all things sparklingly new.

21

WAVE UPON WAVE
OF LOVE

Last summer my family and I spent a few days of vacation at the beach in Florida, which is where I learned the nuances of the beach warning flag system. There is a big difference, for example, between a green flag, which tells swimmers the water is calm and everyone is safe to wade in, and a red flag, which means essentially, "You're an idiot to take on these waves."

Late one morning, Pam and the kids and I headed out to the beach to catch some rays and noticed that it was a red-flag day. While my wife set up shop in the sand, I carefully waded into the water with Abram and Callie, carving out a little boundary line for them on the safe side of where the steep waves seemed to break. "This is as far as I want you guys to go, deal?" I said, even as the water crashed over us and swept under us and made it difficult for us to stand. The ocean's force was so strong, its rhythm so intense, that I quickly adjusted the boundary toward shore a few feet.

I played with my kids in the shallow waters for a while, but the taller waves were so inviting that I just couldn't stay away — maybe it's living in the mountains that makes the ocean's allure so strong. "You two stay inside that line," I shouted toward Abram and Callie, over the whitecaps' noisy interruptions. "I'll be right back."

105

Between their giggles and splashes and screams of joy, they shouted, "Okay, Dad!" and off I went.

No sooner had I made my way to deeper waters than a gigantic wave enveloped me and left me gasping for breath. Pam was reading, the kids were playing, and nobody knew that I had disappeared into a watery cloud. As is so often the case with us Boyds, the family is safe and sound while Dad is out playing the fool. Wiping salt water from my eyes and laughing at the water's force, I wiggled my feet under me to regain my stance, only to have a second wave crash over my head. The riptide was so strong that it dragged me fifteen feet from where I'd been.

I'm a fairly good swimmer, so even that far out, I was able to get my head above water and rally my energies once more. But then—*pow!*—a third wave knocked me under the waterline while seemingly stripping off the top two layers of my skin. I felt my body scrape the sand on the ocean floor and found myself rolled up in the undertow receding from shore. All I could think about was how I—a fat, middle-aged white guy—was going to die such a pitiful death. "Body Surfing Takes Pastor Brady's Life"—what a pathetic way to go!

Actually, I wasn't in real danger. I was just overwhelmed. Time after time I would steady my stance, only to be taken out again.

Persistence. Power. Playfulness. I learned something of God's love that day.

Twenty-two years ago I surrendered my life to Christ. I was compelled to do so not by obligation or fear but rather by God's undeniable love for me. As an early-twentysomething, I still lived at home, and when I came into the kitchen the next morning, I didn't even have to tell my mom what I'd done. She had been praying for my salvation for decades, and she could read it in my eyes. "You're ... *different*!" she said, her hand clasping the smile on her lips.

And was I ever. I felt scrubbed clean and tightly embraced and set on solid ground for the first time in my young life. All these years later I *still* feel the same way. I haven't gotten over how good it feels to be loved by a gracious God.

He loves me. He likes me. He doesn't take his eye off me. He holds me in the palm of his hand, safe and protected and cared for, treating me as a father treats a son.

Son. That's who I became that day I surrendered to Christ. Thankfully, joyfully, it's who I am still.

�֍

Along the way these last twenty-plus years, I have met other Christ followers who, along their own way, also have understood something of the love of God. Something has happened (or didn't happen) in their lives, and they knew it was God's hand at work. The disease was gone, the layoff didn't occur, the rebellious kid came home, things never came to divorce — whatever the circumstance, they could plainly see that God was lovingly pulling strings.

One such man approached me after a Sunday worship service and said that he had been lying in a hospital bed for weeks on end, dealing with complications of his recently diagnosed leukemia. He decided to read through portions of the Bible, in hopes of finding some comfort and hope, and he sensed God directing him to Ephesians 3 — the part about how wide and how deep God's love is. For the first time in forty years, he said, he finally caught the love of his Father. "It came in waves," he explained to me that Sunday. "Wave after wave of his love."

The man said he became so overwhelmed by the reality that he actually prayed for God to stop revealing his love, just so he could catch his breath. "I can't take it anymore!" he said aloud. "Just give me a second here to absorb what you've already shown me!"

Such people have seen God's love, they have sensed his love, they have felt his love, they have *known* it. And those of us who have experienced this immersion into God's love serve him now with all our heart and all our strength, because that's what love compels well-loved people to do. God doesn't dole out teaspoon-fuls of love, nor does he squeeze out a soaked dishrag amount of love, but rather he pours out wave upon wave upon *gigantic, over-whelming wave* of love—washing over us, sweeping under us, sur-rounding us on all sides. It is wide, it is high, it is deep, it is long. It is in us and all around us and never lets us go. It envelops us and consumes us, it sustains us and empowers us. Wherever we've come from and wherever we're going, we can't help but run into God's love.

This messes with the mind, doesn't it? You can't comprehend love so all-encompassing as that. All you can do is receive it.

If there were time in heaven, I think you and I would spend our first billion years there exploring the love of God. This is why heaven is filled to overflowing with worship, because God's mysteries are finally being revealed. And don't you know that questions regarding his great love must be first on everybody's list?

Why the blessing?

Why the favor?

Why the care and concern and regard?

Why the provision?

Why the enjoyment?

Why the compassion?

Why the *grace*?

Until we are bowing before his visible presence, we will never fully grasp the love of God. His love toward us is illogical and irra-tional and would short-circuit our brains if we could ever get close to sorting it out. But lovingly he says, "Between now and then, by the help of my Spirit, may you know my unknowable love."

Isn't that a beautiful thought? It's like being let in on a divine secret, or like discovering the solution to the most complex puzzle in life. God offers us insider info on something that otherwise can't be known.

And so I pray fervently and frequently for people I know who do not yet know Christ. I pray that they would be absolutely *taken out* by wave upon wave upon gigantic, overwhelming wave of God's love. That they would be drawn by God's Spirit to his welcoming side and then be given capacity for understanding just how loved they really are.

We can despise his love and deny it, we can refuse it and discard it. We can mock it and we can snub it. But we can't outswim the love of God. "If grace is an ocean," songwriter John Mark McMillan says, "we're all sinking." I believe that. I really do.

I hope you believe it too.

22

THE DIFFERENCE BETWEEN
SOIL AND DIRT

Two flowerbeds span the front of our Colorado home, one that was planted by professional landscapers before we moved into the house, and one that was tended by an admitted amateur—me. The happy, successful flowerbed boasts rich, dark, vibrant, fertile soil. The plants are thriving, the weeds are minimal, and life is just as it should be in there.

My sad failure of a flowerbed, however, is filled to its brim with useless Rocky Mountain dirt—lifeless, colorless, good for little else besides maybe making bricks. Despite my faithful watering regimen, nothing good is coming from those plants. Not now, not ever. It's just not possible.

Each time I pull into the driveway and eye those flowerbeds—the one that's thriving and the one that's not—I'm reminded that there is a vast difference between being rooted in the richest of soils and being stuck in a pile of hardened dirt. There is only one way my beloved plants will grow, and it won't be by sitting in dirt.

And what is true for shrubberies and foliage is true for the human heart.

I have been reading through the book of Ephesians as a daily discipline, and today I happened upon this sentiment from the

110

apostle Paul, written for a local church he cared deeply about: I pray that you would be "rooted and established in love" (3:17). He might as well have said, "As you go through life, be sure your heart stays near the soil. It won't stand a chance in the dirt."

Love is the soil God knows we need — his perfect, life-giving love.

Sometimes rooting ourselves in love feels easy, like when people are being nice, the skies are blue, and our to-do list gets checked off just as we planned. We saunter through our days, tossing sunshine and lollipops at everyone we meet, thinking, *Isn't it great to be alive?*

But throw a grump, a gray sky, or a grand interruption our way, and it's amazing how unlovely we become. That's precisely why Paul talked in terms of *rootedness*, of *being established*. He knew we needed a permanent solution to the temporary trials we face, and love really is the answer. Whenever we let Christ have his way in our lives, he empowers us to be loving instead of distant, irritated, or mean. When we anticipate challenges in our day and decide to be loving no matter what, we begin to become rooted, which Paul spoke so fondly about.

But the inverse is also true.

When I charge into my day before resurrendering myself to Christ, and as a result trample everyone within six feet of me, I unwittingly settle for plopping my heart into a lifeless pile of dirt. And nothing good comes from dirt, as I say. Not now. Not ever. Not possible.

I'm noticing something about myself these days, which is that even when I am convinced I'm sitting in the rich, fertile soil of God's love, something happens that forces me to acknowledge that I'm not producing as much life as I thought. Nine times out of ten, this dynamic shows up first in my words.

Luke 6:45 says this: "A good man brings good things out of the good stored up in his heart, and an evil man brings evil things out of the evil stored up in his heart. For the mouth speaks what the heart is full of." This is a helpful cue, I think, for our words reveal what's most true about us. If our hearts are rooted in God's love, then what flows from our mouths will be tenderness and kindness, forgiveness, compassion, and grace. If our hearts have been choking on the dirt of bitterness, rage, jealousy, sarcasm, hopelessness, helplessness, or angst, then those dead things can't help but eventually come spewing out. Sure, we might be able to fool each other momentarily, but over time our words will betray our hearts for what they really are. We're either flourishing in soil or dying in dirt—ultimately the truth will be known.

Interestingly, about thirty years after Paul crafted his letter to the Ephesian church, another apostle wrote a similar note. The apostle John, who also had served as the pastor of the church at Ephesus, found himself sitting on an island with a little time on his hands. He decided to write to several churches to encourage them as well as get them back on track. Ephesus was one of these churches, the same group of people whom Paul told to be sure to root and establish themselves in love. They obviously hadn't followed these instructions, because John's letter carried a strong tone.

In Revelation 2:2–5, John wrote, "I know your deeds, your hard work and your perseverance. I know that you cannot tolerate wicked people, that you have tested those who claim to be apostles but are not, and have found them false. You have persevered and have endured hardships for my name, and have not grown weary. Yet I hold this against you: *You have forsaken the love you had at first.* Consider how far you have fallen! Repent and do the things you did at first" (emphasis added).

If there is one thing I never want to do in life, it is to forsake my first love, which is Christ. My life, my health, my hope, my faith, my family, my career, my joy—every good thing I know in this life comes directly from the hand of Christ. Why would I want to walk away from the source of every good thing?

And yet I do. Left to my own oh-so-human devices, I can be petty and hardheaded and cross. I can snap back instead of being gracious; I can brush aside instead of embracing; I can lose heart instead of persisting; I can forgive but be slow to forget. And each time I settle for such smallness, I choose not rich soil for my heart but lifeless dirt.

But then softly, subtly, graciously, gently, my Father appears by my side: "You can return to your first love, Brady. You can point yourself back to me."

Every moment of every day, I can live from my heart's good soil. I can love because I am living well-loved. I can carry grace because I am experiencing God's grace. I can grow into the son God desires me to be, because I am choosing rich soil over worthless dirt.

23

ON FAKE TROPHIES
AND BEARING FRUIT

My daughter, Callie, played soccer this year on a recreational team that got rode like a rented mule every Saturday for four months straight.[12] Callie is a fairly competitive kid and played well during practices and games, but not everyone shared her zest for the sport. In fact, judging by empirical evidence, I can say that there were girls on her team who didn't even know there was a ball on the field.

At the end of the season, Callie and her teammates were invited to a pizza party, along with all of the other teams in her league. The coaches made a big deal about the girls' involvement and then proceeded to hand out trophies to each and every girl. Regardless of whether she was part of a winning team or a losing team, regardless of whether she dribbled like a pro or ever made contact with the ball, every single player received a trophy — the *same* trophy as everyone else.

After we got home that night, I asked Callie why she thought she had received the trophy. She's eleven years old now and can smell a rat. Catching my drift, she said, "It's a great trophy, Dad." (Translation: "Save the teachable moment, old man, and let me have just ten seconds of satisfaction over my award. Deal?")

Ignoring her subliminal message, I asked, "It may *be* great, but don't you wonder what it stands for?"

I think her exact response was ... nothing. Nothing except a shrug of her shoulders on her way out of the room.

If this particular end-of-season trophy ceremony were an isolated incident, maybe I would have let it slide. Probably not, but *maybe* I would have. But the fact is, it's not isolated. Between Pam's and my two kids, our home boasts dozens of medals and trophies, and neither Callie nor her brother, Abram, has ever won a championship of any kind. What's more, they have been involved in soccer, basketball, volleyball, baseball, and tae kwon do and rarely have ever played a game or competed in a match where the score was kept and a winner and a loser determined at the end. But I know the score. *Every* dad knows the score. Every kid probably knows the score too. And my point is this: there is no incentive for my kids to grow more proficient at a sport if they know they will get a trophy, win or lose.

✦✧✦

By the time I was my kids' ages, I knew firsthand the thrill of victory and the agony of defeat. Even younger, as a matter of fact. I remember like it was yesterday missing a jump shot that would have won it all for my third-grade basketball team. Yes, I failed. But the failure didn't scar me. In fact, it compelled me to get better. When I was nine years old, I spent much of my playtime shooting jump shot after jump shot at a basketball rim nailed to a pine tree in my backyard. If there was one thing I was determined to do, it was to prepare myself so that next time I would actually *hit the shot*.

To be fair, I'm sure the people who have been in charge of youth sports for the past decade have legitimate reasons for their approach. There *is* a dark underbelly of competition, and parents' and coaches' ugliness can get unleashed when those adults have to win at all costs. But I'm not convinced that the best solution to these exceptions is to confine our kids to a protective bubble wherein they're never allowed to lose.

I think there's a correlation here, between this ubiquitous sheltered existence and the rash of twentysomethings still living in their parents' basements, with no plans to leave, no plans to achieve, and nothing but time on their hands. They were never challenged as kids, they never learned how to compete, and they have never been forced to recover from failure. Now they find themselves aimless and passionless and weak, while we shake our heads in disbelief.

✢✼✢

Between the years 1940 and 1970, as a country we sent people into space, we invented computers, we created suburbia, and we revolutionized automobile technology. This was a generation of people who had endured a world war, had been challenged in combat, and had parents who had survived the Great Depression, or had survived the depression themselves. Competition was a celebrated part of the culture, and winning and losing mattered deeply. Heroes were honored for their victories, and grace was shown to the defeated. Losers learned tough lessons, and winners had to practice harder to stay on top. It was an age of innovation and persistence in the face of challenge and turmoil and angst. And every member of that generation was better for having prevailed. They understood the value of *improving* and *overcoming*. They didn't need fake trophies to prop themselves up. Hard work was deeply honored, as opposed to limp participation.

As a kid, I used to love the first day of fall. As soon as the air turned crisp, Dad and I would set aside an entire Saturday, and we would busy ourselves chopping wood. The process was rusty for me at first, but over time I found my rhythm, and I learned to be useful as Dad's right-hand man. The work was hard — we would get dirty and sweaty and on occasion bloody too — but I sensed somehow that our effort was important and necessary and good.

And I was right: that cord and a half of firewood would warm our small house all winter long.

Today, whenever I think back on those Saturdays with Dad, I still smell woodchips and chain-saw fumes and productivity. Work was our act of worship—it was our means of bearing fruit.

⚬

A Bible story came to mind the day I challenged Callie about the worth of her trophy. In it, Jesus and his disciples were traveling from Bethany to Jerusalem, when Jesus noticed a fig tree in full bloom. This was good news, since he was hungry. Fig trees always sprout their figs long before their leaves appear, so, assuming there were plenty of figs to eat, he approached the tree. But when he neared, he saw that it was just a bunch of leaves; there wasn't a single fig to be found. "May no one ever eat fruit from you again," he said to the tree (Mark 11:14). What good is a fruitless fruit tree? he figured. It would be better to cut it down.

Similarly, what good is a worker who doesn't work or a producer who doesn't produce? What is the use of a teacher who doesn't teach, a writer who doesn't write, a painter who doesn't paint, an investor who doesn't invest, a pastor who doesn't pastor, a leader who doesn't lead—and a sports team that can't play the sport? Whatever it is we are called to do, we are called to do it as unto God. Sloppiness and laziness and an undisciplined life do *nothing* to honor him. Instead we are to grow and develop and improve and work hard, knowing it is our excellence that points glory his way. He has given us resources to steward—time, talent, money, smarts—and he is a fan of stewardship that is wise.

It is not lost on me that God's first command to humankind was to be *fruitful*. "Be fruitful and increase in number; fill the earth and subdue it," Genesis 1:28 says. "Rule over the fish in the sea and the birds in the sky and over every living creature that moves on the ground." Fruitfulness is what God expects of us, and that comes only by hard work. In other words, we get no trophy for merely showing up. Trophies are reserved for people who are faithful to *work* and who in the end *bear good fruit*. So whether it's the guy digging ditches or the one running cable or the one bagging groceries—or the kid playing soccer on a sunny Saturday afternoon—*everyone* is to view their effort in terms of the fruit they are able to bear.

Let's learn to prize things like diligence and persistence and growth—and let's teach our kids to do the same. Let's let them fail in controlled situations so they know what to do upon meeting opposition when the stakes are *really* high.

24

THE DANGER
OF BEING AT OUR BEST

I had accepted an invitation to speak at a church in Texas one night and was a few hours from addressing the large crowd of people who would gather. Sitting in the corner chair of my hotel room, I found myself praying typical pastor-like prayers. "Help me to speak clearly and effectively," I asked God. "Help me to read the room and respond to your Spirit. You know I can't do this without you."

As I continued praying along these lines, God interrupted my thoughts. *Huh,* I thought. *Imagine that. God has something better to say.*

His message to me would humble and inspire me, convict and compel me all at once: *How about asking not that I would help you but that you would help me tonight?*

I sat there in silence for a moment. God needed help from *me*?

He continued: *I'm already at work in the individual lives in that crowd. Maybe I'm up to something this evening that you could join me in moving along.*

That single momentary encounter forever changed the way I pray. The goal is not for me to perform at my best; it's to partner with the One who is best over all.

✳✻✳

If you were to ask my wife, Pam, how many Sundays I have come home after speaking at worship services all morning and said, "I really hit a home run today!" she would fall apart in laughter. I'm not sure I have *ever* uttered those words, mostly because I'm a guy who struggles with inadequacy far more than with self-importance or pride.

I am grateful for my heritage, because it has formed me into the man I am today. But it hasn't come without its share of discouragements at various points along the way. When I got to college, for instance, it was painfully evident to me that I lacked the credentials and pedigree of my peers. After I graduated from school and entered the workforce, I realized I still wasn't up to snuff: my resumé, my GPA, my leadership experience, my wit—on every conceivable level, I was less-than, not-as-much-as, weak. And then I became a pastor.

When New Life Church, the largest church in the Mountain West region, invited me to come on board as their senior pastor, I distinctly remember raising a suspicious eyebrow toward God. "They *do* know I've never been to seminary, right? And that I'm terribly underqualified? Maybe the search committee didn't do their homework."

As part of the interview process, I had to preach three weeks in a row and then subject myself to a congregational vote. The Monday morning following my third preaching weekend, I told Pam we had to get out of town. "I want to be as far away from here as possible when they tell me I wasn't voted in."

So many insecurities, so little faith that God was at work, so very few occasions in my life when I have tasted being "at my best." But here is why I think this is a blessing and not a curse: I find it's difficult to be concerned with God's great work in the world when I'm busy elevating my own game.

✦✖✦

I have always been captivated by the attitudes and actions of the early followers of Christ. I read the book of Acts and find a group of believers so enthralled with God's will, God's ways, God's work in their world, that they gladly put their own needs aside and pursued his divine mission instead. They were passionate. They were purposeful. They were dead-set on bringing heaven to earth. The last thing on any of their God-focused minds was being "at their best" to wow a crowd.

Peter, one of their leaders, would write that the reason why they were so faithful in their focus was that they possessed a "living hope," and that the living hope they experienced came straight from the resurrection of Christ.

Resurrection people — that's what they were. It's who we can be still today. We can treat the resurrection as a nice, onetime historical event that happened to give us salvation and grace, or we can breathe it in and breathe it out every moment of every day, allowing it to fuel us and fulfill us and align us with the heart of God. It's *his* presence, not ours, that matters. It's *his* power, not ours, that counts. It's *his* work throughout the universe that is changing the world today.

✦✖✦

When I became a Christ follower, God began a good work in me that continues today. But if I'm not careful, I can take my redeemed heart, body, and mind and use them for something other than glorifying God. I can take the miracle he made out of the mess of my life and head back toward "messy" again. I've seen it happen scores of times.

Believers who have walked with Christ for years or decades reach the point where they think they've figured it all out. They lose their love for the mystery and magnificence of God and decide to just go it alone. They sludge their way through the motions and wind up farther and farther from God. They know they have lost their sense of awe, but honestly, what's the big deal? Life is going pretty well, after all. Things can feel good at our best.

✼⚮✼

"Keep me hungry," I've been asking God lately, "for your power, your presence, your work. Help me push past the lesser goal of being at my best and pursue the still-better way of connection, cooperation, and partnership. Let me be a resurrection person today."

25

THE FIRST WORD
OF EVERY GOOD PRAYER

Father, hallowed be your name, your kingdom come.
Give us each day our daily bread. Forgive us our sins,
for we also forgive everyone who sins against us. And
lead us not into temptation.

—LUKE 11:2–4

My mom always has been a woman of prayer. Throughout my childhood, long before the sun was up, I would hear my mom creep from her bedroom to the kitchen to the living room, settle into her chair, and then slowly turn the onionskin pages of her well-worn Bible, one thin sheet at a time. After she read the Scriptures, she would stand up, turn around, kneel in front of her chair, and bury her face in its cushions as she petitioned God in prayer.

Some mornings those prayers took only a few minutes, and sometimes it seemed an hour would go by before my mom was done talking to God on behalf of her family members and friends. As I entered my teenage years, I remember hearing my name called out more often than usual. Even in our small house, where sounds carried easily from room to room, I couldn't always catch what Mom was begging God to do in my life. But given my congenital heart condition, my propensity for adventure, and a burgeoning rebellious streak, I'm sure it had to do with keeping me healthy, keeping me safe, or keeping me from acting like a fool. Probably all of the above.

If there is one reason why I am a pastor today, it is because of the call of God on my life. If there are two reasons, it's that call coupled with my mom's faithful prayers. I had heard people pray thee-and-thou prayers in church throughout my growing-up years, but they never sounded anything like my mom's prayers. There was an unmistakable intimacy between Mom and the One she was praying to, and as I grew old enough to understand spiritual things, I wanted a connection like that of my own.

Whenever I read through the Lord's Prayer in Luke 11, I can't help but recall the prayers of my mother. In the same way that I craved the Father-child relationship my mom relished with God, I think the disciples listening to Jesus pray that day wanted more of what they sensed their Savior enjoying. They too had heard countless prayers uttered to God, and they had prayed thousands themselves. These were men of prayer, men who prized the Word of God enough to memorize the Torah in its entirety. They were men mindful of the Psalms, the heart cries of David and others who *knew* how to communicate with God. And yet that day, upon hearing Jesus pray to God, they were compelled to beg, "Lord, teach us to pray!"

Faithful disciples of Jesus asking to be taught how to pray—it must have seemed to their leader like fish asking to learn how to swim. Still, he didn't rebuke them or blow off their request. Instead he answered them with a gift, the gift of the Lord's Prayer. It was more than a token passage to be memorized and recited. It was a proclamation of Jesus' purpose in coming to the earth and fulfilling God's plan for his life. Through his words, he displayed God as Father and described the life that divine Dad wishes for us all.

He began his prayer with a single word, the word that starts every good prayer. "Father," is what he said.

Father. What an intimate way to start a conversation with the One who holds it all.

By praying to "Father," Jesus wanted his listeners to understand that God was approachable, accessible, relational, and near. But to the faithful Jews gathered before him, the meaning went much deeper than that. Jesus was using language of the exodus fifteen hundred years prior, a fact not at all lost on these men.

In Exodus 4, we find God's chosen people, the Israelites, being held in captivity by Egyptian slaveholders, who are forcing them to labor in the sweltering sun and denying their basic human rights. God is determined to release his people from bondage, so he sends an emissary, Moses, to deliver a message to Pharaoh. Verses 22–23 read, "This is what the LORD says: Israel is my firstborn son." Notice that the reason why God has a right to these people is that they are his daughters and sons, adopted into his family. "Let my son go," God says through Moses, "so he may worship me."

When Jesus began his prayer with "Father," he was affirming his role as Son. In the same way, when you and I call on God as "Father," we imply we are his children. God cannot be Father to us if we don't first accept that we are his daughters and sons.

✦☿✦

Back in the 1990s, it came into vogue to refer to God as "Dad" or "Daddy" or "Pop." I was raised in a very traditional Pentecostal church setting that revered the name of God, and I remember being repulsed whenever I heard Christ followers use these overly familiar terms. I was brought up hearing about how orthodox Jews wouldn't even *speak* God's formal name, *Yahweh*, without covering their heads with their hands. It was a sign of reverence and respect that pointed toward the posture I too was to have. But then I caught the good news of grace, and I began to see my heavenly Father for who he is.

An old photograph featuring former president John F. Kennedy captures the essence of how I now view God. In it, the president is standing to the side of his desk in the Oval Office, tapping his toe and clapping as his young daughter and son jump and dance around the room. Legend has it that the shot was snapped just as the leader of the free world was in the throes of the internationally tense Cuban Missile Crisis, when Russia was trying to establish a missile base in Cuba.

The president and his advisers were pressed to make difficult military and diplomatic decisions, even as they ushered in and out of the Oval Office myriad other world leaders who were seeking an audience with them. During one such meeting, the commander in chief heard the pitter-patter of children's feet outside his doors and cleared his office so he could turn his attention to Caroline and John Jr., if only for a few minutes. Telling, isn't it, that when the weight of the world was on his shoulders, this leader still found time to enjoy his kids.

JFK may have been president of the United States, but to Caroline and John Jr., he was Dad. Those kids didn't see their dad's authority; all they saw was his *access*. President Kennedy wielded the most power of any single individual on the planet, but those closest to him knew that *father* was his favorite role.

It's a fitting metaphor for God. He is all-powerful — and he is Abba. He is all-present — and he is Daddy. He is all-knowing — and he is Papa. Father is his favorite role, and he will grant us an audience, even when we are acting like little children. Perhaps *especially* then. Yes, he commands our deference, but how he loves it when we dance at his feet.

Jesus struck the balance that you and I seek to hit, between intimacy of relationship and insistence on reverence. For although he began his prayer with "Father," he very quickly moved to "hallowed be your name." We can learn to do the same. We can learn to come close, where God desires us to be, while letting that holy ground remind us to humbly slip off our shoes. The combination is critical, because it's at this intersection that freedom begins. When you and I simply say the name of God from our hearts, we take the first step toward freeing whatever needs loosing in life. Amid addictions, obsessions, cravings, compulsions, bondage to shame and sin, we can cry out "Father," knowing he hears us, he sees us, he cares, then "hallowed be your name," knowing he is holy, lofty, righteous, and capable of untethering us from our sin.

We begin every good prayer with the name of the One who is determined to free us because we are his adopted daughters and sons.

26

A PLEA TO
YOUNG PASTORS

There is a real dilemma in the world of church work these days, which is that the people who are planting new churches and thereby entering the role of spiritual father or spiritual mother have grown up in families where they haven't been parented well themselves. They have the right motivation, the right formal training, and the right energy for the job, but what they lack is the simple joy of having lived as a beloved daughter or son.

Recently a group of influential pastors from across the United States assembled to discuss this very issue. I learned a lot that day. Namely, that our country's biggest churches all share a concern about how to properly father young leaders being sent out. Unless something drastic changes, a slew of young pastors stand to fail miserably for the simple reason that people who have never been fathered well tend to make lousy fathers themselves. (Skip to chapter 45 for proof.)

One denomination in particular plans to plant 2,400 churches this year alone, and their leader, who was also in attendance that day, admitted that judging by previous trends, their board expects as many as 70 percent of them to fail within three years. Twenty-four hundred churches planted, and upward of sixteen hundred destined to fail. The math is troubling, to be sure. But surprising? Not at all.

Our churches mirror our culture, and we are presently living in the third consecutive generation of dysfunctional homes in America, meaning that at least one in two families is not operating intact. If the numbers hold, we can assume that half of all of today's church planters hail from single-parent homes. A young, well-educated Christ follower charges ahead, determined to launch the Next Great American Ministry, but he never had a dad. Or if he did, perhaps his father wasn't a good one. The wide-eyed pastor loves God, loves the church, and loves to see kingdom advances made. But he brings with him an orphan spirit that, left unaddressed, will do him in.

⚬

When I knew the time had come for me to leave Gateway Church, where I pastored in the Dallas area, and accept New Life's senior pastor position, a group of loving, godly spiritual fathers there in Texas hemmed me in. They were as determined as I was that I depart not like an orphan but like a son. By their words and by their actions, these elders and colleagues of mine encouraged me to talk candidly with them, listen carefully to their input, pray about the impressions I was receiving, and remain open to course corrections if my plans didn't match up to God's. Perhaps unintentionally, throughout that yearlong process they taught me to lead—and *leave*—from the place of "son."

We have launched four churches since I arrived at New Life, and the straightforward progression I learned from those men has served our departing staff well. Talk, listen, pray, stay open—I learned that these simple steps are what constitute biblical submission, which is more about healthy boundaries and necessary protection than about selfish command and control.

I have always been a fan of the apostle Peter, the straight-shooting, sometimes-fumbling Galilean fisherman who loved to follow Jesus (except when he decided he would deny him a few times) and who was an expert when it came to encouraging people in their faith. I can't read the book of 1 Peter without coming away resolved to be a better leader, a better follower, and a better witness to the watching world.

One passage in particular that always charges me up regarding this issue of submitting to authority is 1 Peter 5:1–5, which says,

> To the elders among you, I appeal as a fellow elder and a witness of Christ's sufferings who also will share in the glory to be revealed: Be shepherds of God's flock that is under your care, watching over them—not because you must, but because you are willing, as God wants you to be; not pursuing dishonest gain, but eager to serve; not lording it over those entrusted to you, but being examples to the flock. And when the Chief Shepherd appears, you will receive the crown of glory that will never fade away.
>
> In the same way, you who are younger, submit yourselves to your elders.

This simple set of verses served as a playbook for my Gateway friends, and two big ideas that show up here led their thoughts, their words, their actions, and their reactions. And they and I were better for it.

First, Peter put the onus on church leaders ("elders," he called them, which just means those people who are wiser and more mature in their faith) to set an example for the congregations they lead. "Hey," he said, "I'm one of you. I'm a ministry leader too and know how tough it can be. But before God and the people I lead, I will show by my words and by my actions what it means to live as a chosen son."

I can't ask anything of people I lead unless I'm first committed to caring for them, guiding them, and protecting them. The day I quit caring for, guiding, and protecting the people I am called to pastor is the day I ought to resign, both for their sake and for mine.

Peter said, in essence, "Now that we're clear on what the leaders must do, let me get to the point I was really trying to make. The reason why leaders are to lead well is to give followers something to follow."

What the elders of Gateway Church showed me — and what I hope I am showing to my staff at New Life now — is that when leaders set a fatherly example and followers are willing to learn how to be sons, God is honored, the church is strengthened, and scores of orphans finally find their way home. And it all comes down to one idea: *submission.* Talk, listen, pray, stay open — it's how we live lives that are submitted to God, and it's how we cooperate in ministry with people wiser in the faith.

Talk.

I will ask for advice before I act, instead of asking for forgiveness afterward.

Listen.

I will pay attention to the thoughts and requests you convey, and will hear you with nonjudging ears.

Pray.

I will seek God regarding what you have to say. I will cultivate a lifestyle of talking with my Father — asking questions, stilling myself in anticipation of answers, relishing divine dialogue.

Stay open.

Perhaps most important, I will change direction when necessary. I will keep an open mind regarding my plans in life, and I will respond with grace when things don't go my way.

※

Submission is the unsung source of strength in the pastoral vocation. As I've met with each of New Life's dynamic young church-planting pastors before they've taken flight, I have begged them to remember that they will have only as much spiritual authority as the spiritual authority they submit to. If they insist on being renegades, operating with an independent mind and heart, God won't entrust to them much authority; he won't send his sheep their way.

But if they will allow spiritual fathers to come into their lives and will candidly engage with them, if they will pray earnestly and respond graciously as God's will is done in their lives, they will be invited to fulfill the role of "Dad" to plenty of fortunate daughters and sons.

27

YURI LITE STAR

Years ago I met a man named Yuri Lite Star. I figured a name like that must come with a pretty good story, and as I got to know him better, the tale that spilled out didn't disappoint. For starters, he had been raised on a hippie compound in Hawaii. Which added up, in my view. I had sort of envisioned anyone named Yuri Lite Star hailing from a bunch of indolent types living on a beach. Wouldn't you?

Nine months before Yuri's birth, his mother was on a road trip in California—where she lived at the time—with a few fellow hippies to buy some marijuana, when she had a one-night stand with one of her traveling companions. After the deed was done, she looked at her bedfellow and said, "I am pregnant; I just know it." According to her, the whole room had lit up during their intimate encounter, and, dismissing the possibility that it was simply the drugs causing her psychedelic experience, she took that as a sign that her womb now bore a child. Interestingly, she was right.

✦✼✦

Eventually Yuri's mother—as well as her four children, including the one growing inside her belly—took up residence in Hawaii with some of her hippie friends. While she was sitting beside the ocean one night, alone and captivated by the stars above, the name Yuri Lite Star came to her. Her other three children had typical Western names, and nobody in the family had the last name Star. It had been something of a vision, she later explained to her son, the first in a brand-new lineage, a baby boy who would be called Yuri Lite Star.

As you might expect, given the environment Yuri grew up in, by eight years old he was smoking pot, by twelve he was selling, and by sixteen he was a full-fledged devotee of the surfer-hippie lifestyle, with no formal education, no commitments, and not a care in the world. But he wouldn't stay that way for long.

At seventeen, things changed radically for Yuri. He happened to meet a pastor who spoke of love and grace and God, he surrendered his life to Jesus Christ, and then, after being encouraged by his newfound friend to get off the Island and attend school, he relocated to Dallas, Texas, where he attended Bible school at Christ for the Nations. While there, Yuri began growing curious about his roots. Maybe hunting down his MIA father could provide the familial anchor Yuri so desperately desired. With the aid of the Internet and a few scattered memories from his mom, Yuri eventually was able to track down his dad, who by now was a successful video engineer living in California. Around the same time, Yuri received a job promotion that required him to travel to California. The meeting finally was going to happen.

Yuri made his way across the country and showed up in the lobby of his father's office building. Later he told me that despite the crush of businesspeople entering and exiting the premises, when he saw one man in particular step off the elevator, Yuri knew instantly that it was his dad. Clearly, it wasn't because the two resembled each other—instead of boasting dark skin and brown eyes, as Yuri did, the older man had blond hair and blue eyes. But confident in his gut feeling, he approached the man, verified the man's identity, and said, "Hi, I'm Yuri."

Although Yuri and his dad did maintain contact after that initial meeting, nothing earth-shattering happened from there. But this is what gets me about Yuri's story: this young man with no known heritage, no support system, and no role model for living as a spiritual son wound up discovering God as Dad, marrying a godly woman who was clear about her identity in Christ, raising four strong and servant-hearted sons of his own, and starting a successful business from scratch. He was determined to pass on the worthy heritage he himself had never enjoyed.

Yuri's name may be unique, but his story certainly is not. In my line of work, I come across far too many "Yuri Lite Stars" who don't have a happy ending. Unlike the real Yuri, they drift through life anchorless and rudderless and desperate for security and peace. They don't know who they are. They don't know where they are going. The only thing they're sure of is that something seems unsettled in their soul.

✕

I came across a book several years ago written by a man named Marc Pittman. Marc is the father of Cole Pittman, who played football for the University of Texas but had his stellar collegiate career cut short by a fatal car accident during one of his trips from his home in Louisiana back to school in Austin, Texas. *Raising Cole* is a tribute from a loving father to a son, but it is also a testimony to God's faithfulness, for Marc Pittman wasn't shown how to be a loving father by his own dad. "My father never told me that he loved me," Marc writes, "and never showed me any affection except the occasional pat on the head.... How I wished I could have heard him say it just once."[13]

But that unmet longing didn't stop Marc from raising Cole

and Cole's younger brother in a loving and affirming environment. "Often I hear people talk about how they don't grow close to their kids because they never had a father to learn from," he says. "You don't need a father to teach you. All you need is a heart, a resolve, and one simple guideline: Be the father you always wanted to have."[14] Insofar as that heart is surrendered to Christ and that resolve is fueled by faith, this man is onto something that is a game changer for us all.

There is good news for every Yuri Lite Star and Marc Pittman out there: Regardless of the kind of father we know here on earth, our Dad in heaven never abandons or mistreats us. And once we accept our place in our heavenly Father's family, we will find all the role model we need for leading our children well.

28

DEATH TO
THE SPINNING GLOBE

When I first arrived at New Life, one of the church's ministries I was most excited about engaging with was the World Prayer Center. Located on the same campus as the church, the center was established in 1998 to give individuals and groups a place to intercede on behalf of their friends and families, the community of Colorado Springs, and every nation across the globe. Surrounding the center is a beautiful prayer walk, marked by nearly a hundred full-size flagpoles on which the banners of every country are periodically flown, not as some sort of geopolitical endorsement of the power systems in our world but as a simple reminder for lovers of Jesus to pray.

Inside, there is a series of private rooms that people can reserve—quiet spaces for personal retreats, dedicated prayer times, small group meetings, and more. Positioned on many of the walls are large TV monitors, which scroll worldwide prayer requests in nonstop fashion. And then there is the World Prayer Center chapel, a giant room bordered by tall windows, all boasting a gorgeous Pikes Peak view. For more than a decade, New Lifers have gathered in that chapel to sing and speak their praise to God. Conferences have been held there. Prayer meetings have borne fruit there. Worship services have nearly raised the roof. The chapel isn't any ordinary room; geographically it's the *ethos* of the people of New Life Church.

Which should have been my first clue regarding the resistance I'd meet upon suggesting we change things up.

＊✄＊

It all started during my interview process for the role of senior pastor. I was in town for a clandestine meeting with the search committee, and following our scheduled time together, I was given a private tour of the campus. As soon as my hosts and I set foot in the World Prayer Center, I knew I was in for a treat. I had never been in a world prayer center. I had never even heard of such a thing. But the spirit of the place was magnetic to me. I loved the motivation of praying for every nation's people to surrender to Christ. We wandered the halls and peeked into prayer rooms, and I felt a sense of reverence in the place, knowing just how many prayers had been prayed. Then we headed to the chapel — which is where everything went downhill.

In the center of the otherwise-lovely room was the ugliest, gaudiest, most gigantic world globe I'd ever seen. It must have been fifteen feet in diameter, which means it completely blocked the view of the mountain. To make matters worse, it *moved*. I stood there for a minute, just taking it all in, which is when I noticed that every time the globe slowly rotated to North America, it brought with it a nails-on-chalkboard screech. *Creeeeeak! Creeeeeak! Creeeeeeeeeak!*

I thought about suggesting a little WD-40, but then a better idea came to mind. Tugging out the little notepad I had slipped into my coat pocket earlier that day, I grabbed my pen and under a list I had started of first-month initiatives I would be sure to tackle, should I wind up getting the job, I jotted down, "Kill the spinning globe."

Then I underlined *kill* three times.

Here's how the deed would get done: I would hire a dump truck to cart the obnoxious orb to Interstate 25, the freeway that traverses the state of Colorado and beyond. I would have the driver lift the bed of that truck as fast as possible, and I would cackle as the globe flew down the road. It would roll its way south of the Springs to Pueblo and Walsenburg and Trinidad. It would cross the state line to New Mexico, passing Raton and Santa Fe, Albuquerque and Socorro and more. It would bounce past Truth or Consequences and Las Cruces before taking one giant leap across South Texas and drowning in the Gulf of Mexico.

At *last* I could exhale relief, knowing that a key task had been checked off my list. Too bad not everybody would share my enthusiasm.

The day I informed the staff and congregation that our beloved spinning globe was going the way of cassette tapes and tucked-in shirts was the day I experienced near revolt. Scores of conversations later I convinced the would-be dissidents that yes, I still believed in prayer. Yes, I still thought the World Prayer Center was a uniquely marvelous place. Yes, I loved the world.

I. Just. Couldn't. Take. That. Globe.

Today, if you visit the center, you will enjoy a beautifully globe-free experience, thanks to a little heavy lifting and a church that was (eventually) willing to change.

I learned something important about the kingdom of God as that globe was bid a not-so-fond farewell: we will never be open to God's work in this world unless we open our arms wide to change. Throughout the pages of Scripture, our heavenly Father assures us that he is not merely *occasionally* at work bringing beauty from ashes, strength from weakness, hope from despair, faith from fear; he is *always* at work doing these things. Which means things around us are constantly in a state of beautiful, life-altering flux.

It intrigues me that Jesus arrived on planet Earth with the very same motivation the Pharisees had: seeing the kingdom of heaven come down to our neck of the woods. They must have been furious, then, when this so-called Messiah refused to follow their rules. "What? He won't require that we go to the temple for cleansing? What? We no longer have to sacrifice animals for the forgiveness of our sins? What? Salvation is as easy as repenting, believing, and receiving and requires nothing by way of good works?"

What?

Grace was in their grasp, but the Pharisees didn't have eyes to see. They missed out on a life-changing moment because Jesus wasn't doing things the way they had always been done.

✂

In all honesty, I have no idea how God feels about New Life's spinning globe. Perhaps I should add this to the list of questions I want to ask when we meet face-to-face. But here is what I do know: Sometimes the old way is not the best way. Some things are destined for dismantling, and sometimes you're the best person for the job.

Grace is free access to a dump truck, ready to help get rolling what needs to be rolled. The stagnant status quo can't harm us, if we're faithful to show it the door and move on.

29

HYPE VERSUS
THE HOLY SPIRIT

A couple of years ago I began to follow on Twitter a dozen or so high-profile pastors whose ministries I deeply respect. Every few days, I would receive their 140-character updates and would be excited to read what they wrote. Until I actually read what they wrote.

Several months into this receive-and-read trend, my enthusiasm nearly fizzled to nil. Almost every update from almost every pastor I was following was filled to overflowing with hype. In anticipation of that Sunday's worship service, they would tout the "Super Bowl of all Sundays," "the megamonster of all sermons," "a weekend that promised to be *off the chain*" (according to Urban Dictionary: "a great deal of fun"). "I can't think of another time I have been more excited about preaching a message," one pastor wrote. "Miss Sunday's service at your own peril!!!"

Sadly, the exclamation-point-laden hype wasn't coming from just one person; it was flowing freely from *many* mouths, deflating my heart. Because what happens when the service *isn't* megamonster?

How *can* it be, week after week?

✦✖✦

I enjoy reading about church history, and if I were to peg the central characteristics of church gatherings in the first century, they would be *nonhyped, nonfrantic, unrushed*. Worship was a lifestyle, not an overly promoted activity occurring one hour, one morning a week. Things were simple. Prayers were meaningful. People were fully dependent on the Spirit of God.

It's the polar opposite of how we operate today, in our infamous glitz-and-gratification culture. We favor microwaves over Crock-Pots and sex appeal over substance. We like it fast and easy and *now* ... and preferably at little cost to us. As it relates to the churchgoing experience, we rush in on a Sunday morning—fifteen minutes late at best—scurry to find a seat, get antsy after sixty minutes, and rush right back into our day. We sing songs with lines like "wait upon the Lord" and bob our heads in apparent agreement, even as we silently wonder how much longer the song set will last.

We are moving far too fast to hear it, of course, but still God whispers, *Be still.*

Relax.

Linger.

Drop the hype, please.

Let me show up and do my work.

It would be easy to blame church congregations for the madness that has consumed our gatherings these days, except that from what I see from their pastors, we're *conditioning* them to behave this way. We hype and promote and position and tweet and inadvertently create pews full of consumers instead of devoted worshipers of God. I once heard it said that leaders who don't teach their congregations to worship must entertain them week in and week out. So true. We hype-ers are setting up our people to expect an experience, instead of teaching them to *encounter* their Lord.

✦✧✦

I spent some time on a beach in Florida following my heart surgery this summer, and one of the books I read while there was Eugene Peterson's late-1980s *Working the Angles*. It took only two pages for conviction to cause tears to well up in my eyes. "The pastors of America have metamorphosed into a company of shopkeepers," he writes, "and the shops they keep are churches. They are preoccupied with a shopkeeper's concerns — how to keep the customers happy, how to lure customers away from the competitors down the street, how to package the goods so that the customers will lay out more money."[15]

Ugh.

I don't want that to be me. My goal as a pastor who gets up in front of a fellowship every weekend is to display passion that comes from having been in the presence of God, instead of the slickness that always surfaces when you've been sucked into the latest trend.

I read on, and I resonated deeply with Peterson's call to pastors to return to the three basic acts critical to pastoral ministry: prayer, reading Scripture, and giving spiritual direction to people in need. It's a recipe for hype-free pastoring at its best, fully relying not on a big personality but on the very big Spirit of God.

It sounds good, but if you have ever actually tried to pursue this three-pronged prescription, you know just how tough it can be. Prayer and Bible reading aren't exactly celebrated these days; they are certainly not quantifiable, as attendance and tithes are. But God says, *I see the worthwhile contribution you're making. This is how I want you to do church.*

Proverbs 29:25 lays out the ultimate case against hype: "Fear of man will prove to be a snare," it says, "but whoever trusts in the LORD is kept safe." If only we could catch this idea. Hyping to garner favor from our congregations will disable us, destroy us, and cause us to keep trying to trump ourselves week after week. Trusting in the Lord protects us from all that, keeping us humble and grounded and safe.

30

DAD'S DISTINCT WHISTLE

When I was six years old, the town where my family lived, Logansport—about thirty miles south of Shreveport—hosted the Louisiana State Fair. And when the fair arrived, it was a very big deal. People from every direction trailered their cows and pigs and horses across county lines, enormous carnival rides were constructed seemingly overnight, and twenty acres of once-deserted fairgrounds boasted fried foods and flashing lights.

One Saturday night, my parents, my brother, my sister, and I loaded into the car, drove the half hour from our house to the grounds, and prepared for a memorable night. And it would be memorable, all right. But in ways I didn't expect.

Soon after we arrived, my family and I were walking up the midway, where all the action was. People were barking at me from every side. "Step right up!" "Come give us your best shot!" "Test your brute strength!" "Fresh funnel cake, son!" For a six-year-old, it was sensory overload. My eyes were sponges, trying in vain to soak it all in.

Last I knew, my parents were right behind me and, as was customary, I was out leading the charge. But the allure of the promoters was too tempting, and eventually I wandered away. I was losing myself in the sights, the sounds, the smells, the pizzazz ... and then—*gulp*—I was totally lost myself.

I glanced to my right and then to my left, hoping to spot my mom or my dad. I turned all the way around in place, and still they were nowhere to be found. My heart raced and my eyes pooled with tears. *They had to be here somewhere, didn't they? Hadn't they noticed I wasn't around?*

I pinballed back and forth across the midway for what felt like hours, hoping, *praying* for a familiar face. And then, just as I was about to completely fall apart, I heard, rising above the chaotic noise, the whistle I knew and loved. *Dad!* I would have known that sound anywhere. Faint at first, but then louder, louder—beautifully, wonderfully louder. Although I couldn't see him yet, I knew my dad was near.

⚇

Growing up in Louisiana, I found it wasn't uncommon to be surrounded by people who were missing a few teeth here and there. My dad actually possessed a full set, but his front tooth had a small chip in it, which enabled him to whistle like nobody else I'd heard. His buddies used to ask him why he didn't pay to have the tooth fixed, to which he replied, "Got my bird dogs trained to this whistle, boys. I'd be crazy to mess up our deal."

Back at the fair, that whistle transformed terror into tranquility in my tender heart, as I realized I hadn't been left alone. As his whistle neared, I spun to catch sight of his tall frame a few yards away, and with that simple sighting, my heart rate returned to normal. Dad had not taken his eye off me; he had been watching me the entire time. He let me wander just far enough to teach me a lesson I would not soon forget. Then, like any good father, he picked the perfect time to call me home.

⚇

A favorite Scripture of mine is Psalm 23, which begins with these well-known words: "The LORD is my shepherd, I shall not want. He makes me lie down in green pastures; He leads me beside quiet waters. He restores my soul; He guides me in the paths of righteousness for His name's sake."

But then comes verse 4. "Even though I walk through the valley of the shadow of death," it says, "I fear no evil, *for You are with me*" (NASB, emphasis added).

God's "with-ness" is what we are seeking when life feels uncertain and unsteady. The knowledge that he is near to us is what we need when we have lost our way.

✦✂✦

This past year has been stuffed with challenges for nearly every person I know. The economy continues to tumble, jobs are few and far between, marriages are under attack, hardheaded kids insist on going their own way, diseases wrack seemingly healthy bodies—the list goes on and on.

The pace of life only intensifies, and peace seems elusive at best. But amid the swirl of hardship, I have sensed God saying to me, *Brady, people are overwhelmed by the circumstances they face, because they've stopped believing I am near. Don't give way to panic. And tell others to stop panicking too. I am closer than the air you're breathing, and my presence brings all the power you need.*

I have talked with scores of believers who are being swept up by anxiety as they hit these waves of challenges, because they can't seem to feel God anymore. They don't have the same goose bumps they would get while singing catchy worship tunes on Sunday morning, and they wonder where God has gone.

If you are feeling a similar disconnect, please know that your Father has not fled the scene. Stop your pinballing and quiet your spirit, and you will hear the whistle you need. *I'm here,* God says. *I see you. I am committed to your good. My arm is not too short to help you, and with me you will never be lost.*

✳

Lately, Pam and I have been teaching Abram and Callie what it means to quiet our house, even if it's just for a few fleeting minutes each day. We walk through our home turning off every noise-maker we can find—TVs, stereos, gaming machines, ceiling fans, the washer, the dryer, and the lamp that's possessed with a weird buzz—and we sit in silence, alone with our thoughts.

We are not trying to make our kids monks. (Trust me, there's no real risk of that.) But we do want them to learn to appreciate silence and stillness so they can quickly tune in to the presence of God. It's a helpful practice for you and me both, I think, to get perfectly quiet before God. He's near and he's eager to fill us with the peace and courage we need.

I think I hear him whistling now.

31

SONS AND DAUGHTERS LEAN IN

I was born with a congenital heart defect requiring surgery when I was an infant, the same surgery that many other kids underwent that year but didn't survive. The procedure performed on me provided a patch, not a cure, which means that for more than four decades, I have wrestled with this weakness, this less-than-perfect heart. In short, I know my way around a cardiologist's office, and I have been closely acquainted with fear. The docs have told me all along that I would need several more surgeries throughout my life. This past summer, their predictions came true.

I was aware, as I checked into the hospital two months ago, that I was going to have my pulmonary valve replaced with a cow's aorta about the size of my pinky. (Hold the bovine jokes; New Lifers have covered them all.) What I wasn't thoroughly briefed on was the day-before-surgery tests.

Twenty-four hours prior to my open-heart surgery, I was put under anesthesia while doctors scoped my heart through a vein in my leg and tried to thrust me into cardiac arrest. It's not that they didn't like me; they were just curious as to whether I had any dangerous rhythms in my heart. And I did. Wouldn't you know it: the day before massive surgery, and my body decides to die. The chief surgeon evidently brought me back to life with those magic paddles, even as I slept soundly, unaware of my untimely demise. Which, incidentally, is exactly how I wish to die, when I do it for good someday.

So the docs got what they were after: a tip-off to some dangerous rhythms that they would try to correct when they went in for the valve. Relieved that I had survived pre-op, I flipped over sometime around midnight and tried to get some sleep.

+✂+

The day of surgery, I woke at 5:00 a.m. The nurse covering my wing knew it was a big day for me but seemed unsure of what to say as she entered my room. All I noticed was no breakfast accompanying her; no food, no drinks, no exceptions. I had been told these were the rules. "You okay?" she finally offered, to which I nodded and confidently said, "Yeah."

And I was. My family had been in to pray with me. I had spent time alone with God. All that was left was for the doctor to wield a knife and then for all of us to wait for the new me to kick in.

A few minutes later I was wheeled into a prep room by a medical tech wearing scrubs. He leaned over my gurney, caught my eye meaningfully, and said, "Doing okay?"

Again I said, "Yeah." Then added, "Why? Am I not supposed to be?"

I was later told that I seemed "too at peace," which is not at all characteristic of someone about to undergo the surgery I soon would face. The truth was that God was sustaining me, whispering moment-by-moment assurances my way. And his voice would prove key to my making it through a very tough day.

+✂+

My surgeon would describe my operation as "textbook," which gave my family and me all sorts of reasons to celebrate. Until five days later, when I was asked to subject myself to the same test I'd undergone (and failed) pre-op. My cardiology team needed to know if they had corrected the problem or if my rhythms still presented a risk. Back under anesthesia I went, back through my leg vein they went, and *boom*, right back into cardiac arrest. More panic, more paddles, more prayers that I would come back to life.

When I woke up, a sober-faced surgeon was staring at me, grave results on his lips: "Brady, I want to shoot straight with you. You still have extremely dangerous rhythms in your heart. Twenty percent of people with your same condition have a fatal episode within twelve months of diagnosis. The odds aren't great."

No kidding, Doc, I was thinking. *Thanks for the real day-brightener here.*

He continued. "But there is some good news. If you will let me implant a defibrillator, you will have a 99.9 percent chance of surviving anything that dares to come your way."

I am not an expert mathematician, but I knew which route to take. Forty-four years old with two amazing kids and a gorgeous wife I'm crazy about. A church I love serving with, and at least half a life left to live. "Sold," I said with something approximating a smile. "When can we get it done?"

As I look back on last summer, I realize that the surgical experience I have come through was just as much emotional and spiritual in nature as it was physical. I thought I approached life with a fair amount of boldness, but the fear I felt this time around threatened to do me in. Granted, it's tough when all you hear are messages of doom: *Risky surgery. Fatal rhythms. Not good odds.* I thought back on the forms I had been asked to sign prior to my pre-operation procedures and the heart surgery itself: "Chance of death," it read in a big, bold font, solidifying what I already knew to be true.

Fear seems the only reasonable path to walk when circumstances are unnerving and grim.

Case in point: The day I checked into the hospital, I drove up to the valet-parking area and waited my turn. Six or seven men and women waiting for rides to take them wherever they were going were sitting on various benches, and every one of them had a portable oxygen tank in tow. It was like a setup straight from hell, orchestrated just for Brady Boyd. "That will be you," the Enemy whispered to me. "You're going to be that guy with the oxygen tank, the guy who can't breathe well or talk well or *live* well."

In less than a minute's time, I had let Satan convince me that following my surgery, I would never preach again or travel again or take my kids hiking up the Spruce Mountain trail. "You will be weak and frail and sickly," he said, "spending your days in bed, barely alive."

I distinctly remember entering the hospital with a pair of demoralizing thoughts in mind: *They're not going to be able to fix me. This is as good as I'll ever feel.*

But then the still, small, subtle voice of God: *I'm here. I love you. And your future is in my hands.* Simple words, maybe. But simple words that stilled my soul.

✦✼✦

The truth about sons is this: even when the outlook is bleak, they lean into their Father, not their fear. As I read it, the most common command offered in Scripture is, "Fear not." The second most common? "Fear God." I think there is something to this duo. I don't have to be governed by fear, crippled by fear, consumed by fear, or focused on fear. The only fear I am to know is fear of God, and *that* fear is what leads me to peace.

This is more than mere theory to me. When you find yourself in a valley that leads to death, it's important to know you are not alone. I have talked to scores of young believers who panic when they hit their first spiritual speed bump, because life suddenly doesn't seem right. They lack the spiritual electricity that sizzles when things are easy and enjoyable and fun. But they haven't yet walked with Christ long enough to realize that God is as close to us during times of trial as he's ever been, and he is eager to show us the way out.

✦✼✦

Recently a young man asked me a great question. "Brady," he said, "how do you know it's *God's* voice you're hearing, as opposed to your own thoughts that run through your mind?"

I asked if the guy was married—he wasn't—and smiled as I let an analogy answer for me.

"Let's say you've been married fifteen years," I said. "You're out running errands, and your cell phone rings. For some reason, no number shows up on the screen, but you decide to answer it anyway. Your wife of fifteen years says, 'Hey, honey,' and in reply you say, 'Who is this?'"

"No matter how kind your wife is," I continued, "I guarantee you're in trouble, my friend."

When a couple has been wed for fifteen years, an *expectation of intimacy* exists. I have been married to Pam for twenty-two years now, and I guarantee I don't have to ask who is calling when it's her on the other end of the line. I am familiar with that woman's voice. I know that woman's voice. I enjoy it. I treasure it. I *crave* it.

How do I know God's voice from every other voice out there, including the one in my own head? I am familiar with it. I enjoy it. I treasure it. I crave it. Having thousands of conversations across many, many years yields intimacy between a loving Father and a son who's leaning in.

"My sheep listen to my voice," Jesus said, referring to his daughters and sons and implying that he is, in fact, speaking. There are nearly seven billion people on this planet of ours, and he wants to talk to us, every one. He wants to replace fear with confidence, anxiety with peace, insecurity with affirmation, weakness with strength. He really does. He really *will*, when we lean in to hear what he says.

32

THE KINGDOM
IS FOR KIDS

This month I became the parent of a teenager. My son, Abram, turned thirteen, and at eleven years old, his sister, Callie, is right on his heels. I know it's fashionable for parents of teens to shake their heads and roll their eyes and pray mockingly, "God help us all," but Pam and I don't feel that way about entering this season of parenthood. We're actually *excited* to see what God does. We love the idea that our kids are becoming young adults, and that we are handed the honor of helping them walk well as they enter that stage.

At the same time, we recognize that parenting teenagers is not for the faint of heart. It takes skill. It takes patience. It takes sincere and consistent prayer. And if there is one prayer my wife and I have been praying here lately, it's that God would show us how to help our kids keep their childlike innocence, even as they leave their childish days behind. We have been praying the same prayer for ourselves, actually — that as Pam and I continue walking with Christ, we would become like kids again, full of life and love and fun. This is more than a nostalgic longing for gentler and simpler days; we know it's the only way we will experience the kingdom of God. Jesus said as much himself.

✦✕✦

It was an ordinary day. Jesus was hanging out with his disciples, explaining his Father's will and ways through parables and exhortations and by modeling behavior they could emulate. While he was instructing his closest followers in the way of righteousness, people from the crowd that always seemed to gather when Jesus was around started bringing their kids to him, asking him to hold them and bless them. They wanted the touch of the Messiah on their children's lives, and they boldly made their requests known.

In our day and in our culture, children are celebrated. Women are given baby showers long before their little ones show up. In honor of the kids in our lives, we have baby dedications and birthday parties and treat Christmastime like our own personal toy drives. But in Jesus' day, this wasn't the case. Children were worthless—literally. They were valued as nothing more than property because they couldn't yet pull their own weight; they couldn't yet *produce*. They were like weeds: they sucked up valuable resources but offered nothing fruitful in return.

It was against this cultural landscape that these children were handed to Christ—which explains why the disciples were so annoyed. The twelve men rebuked the moms and dads who had the audacity to step into Jesus' presence with their little weeds. But no sooner had the disciples done so than they were handed a rebuke of their own. "Let the little children come to me," Jesus said to them. "And do not hinder them, for the kingdom of God belongs to such as these" (Luke 18:16).

He continued, "Truly I tell you, anyone who will not receive the kingdom of God like a little child will never enter it" (v. 17).

It's the verbs in that last part that always grab my attention: *receive* and *enter*. Unless we receive God's kingdom in the spirit of a child, we will never take up residence there.

✦✕✦

Thanks to the two youngest members of the Boyd clan, I have been schooled on childlikeness this past decade or so. And my observations have taught me why the kingdom belongs to kids. Kids are dependent, for starters. They rely on someone else in order to meet their every need. Kids are also *fun*. What's more, they make for good followers—at least they do most of the time. For years, Pam and I have noticed that wherever we are in the house, our kids tend to migrate there too. They *follow* us. They mimic our dialect, our mannerisms, our habits, our idiosyncrasies—as well as our likes and dislikes. In our house, this means donning jerseys for the LSU Tigers and the Dallas Cowboys, and not for anyone else.

Kids also trust easily that what an authority figure tells them is true. And conversely, kids are honest—again, *most* of the time. Let me put it this way: If you're a woman, never ask a kid if a particular outfit makes you look fat. If it does, you will hear about it, with no sugarcoating and no regrets.

Kids love being home. There is something built into the heart of a child that makes them love the predictability of home. Our family loves going on vacation and taking day trips and running around town, but there is nothing like coming home to what is familiar and comfortable and *us*.

Kids see the best in other people and believe that others' motives are nothing but pure. This dynamic changes once they hit the teenage years, of course, when their cynicism tends to soar. But during those wide-eyed childlike years, they see heroes everywhere they go.

Kids also hope for the future. They anticipate great things ahead, whether it's next week's picnic in the park or the day they will become the firefighter or astronaut or teacher or whatever it is they dream of being.

I watch my kids navigate life with spirited childlikeness and nod at Jesus' claim that "children are the kingdom's pride and joy" (Luke 18:17 MSG). And I'm finally beginning to understand why.

If only I were as dependent on God as my kids have been on my wife and me. If only I were as fun as my kids—if only *all* believers were so fun. Some Christ followers I know were far more fun when they were lost, truth be told. Yes, now they have peace and joy and assurance of salvation. They have hope at their beck and call. But they just forget to let their faces know that it's okay to smile once in a while. It's okay to have some fun.

There are other childlike qualities I would do well to adopt as my own, such as following with unabashed enthusiasm or trusting at every turn. Being honest in big ways and small ways alike. Being comfortable just hanging out with Dad. Choosing to believe the best about people. Staying hopeful about the future I see.

I know it's not manly for a grown man like me to think of himself as a child. But Jesus was speaking to twelve *men* that day when he was asked to bless babies from the crowd. And despite how manly they may have been, he was asking them to be *kids*.

"Receive the kingdom like a little child," Jesus said in essence to his disciples—and to us. "Come with your dependence, your followership, your sense of fun. Come with your honesty, your optimism, your trust. Come with as much hope as you can fit in your grip, knowing my plans for you will prosper you all your days. Come to me with childlike wonder for who I am and for what I can do. And come with arms wide open, prepared to receive the kingdom of God."

＊♋＊

I think the reason why God tells us we have to become like children to enter his domain is because his kingdom is something that cannot be earned; it must simply be received. And most adults I know are atrocious receivers. They feel guilty, they refuse, they try to repay; simply receiving is not in their makeup. God knew that in order for us to position ourselves for grace, we would have to grow down, not grow up. Let me show you what I mean.

I have a friend who never lets me pay for anything. I should be thankful for friends like this, right? Actually, I am not.

He and I were on a road trip together recently, and when we were an hour or so from our destination, he pulled off the interstate to get some gas. By this point in the trip, he had already purchased three tanks of gas. I had tried to buy the last two for him but was denied each time. This time I insisted. His reply was, "Absolutely not."

After we were back on the road, I glanced at him and said, "You know, I don't think you've caught grace."

We are close enough friends that I knew I could shoot painfully straight.

"What do you mean?" he said, feigning offense.

"You've caught the idea of giving," I explained, "but grace is a far different thing. Giving, if not done properly, is a tool used for controlling other people's lives. But grace is always humble. Grace says, 'I will receive and just say thanks.'"

Kids intuitively understand this idea. How hard is it to give a gift to a kid? Imagine this exchange, between my two kids and me:

(Me) "Hey, guys! Guess what? I picked up a little something for each of you today. Want to know what it is?"

(Callie) "Nah, I'm too busy right now."

(Abram) "I can't take a gift from you, Dad, because I didn't get you anything."

Yeah, right.

Take any kid in any country on any continent in the world and tell them you would like to give them a gift, and you'd better have something to hang on to, because you're about to be plowed right down. Kids *love* to get gifts. They are born with open arms. They know beautifully well how to *receive*.

They don't concern themselves with repayment plans or schemes to give in return. They simply throw the doors wide open and say, "For *me*? Hot diggity dog!" *This* is the response God asks of us, the response of a wonder-filled child. "Thank you, Father, for your great gift of grace. I receive it with open arms."

There's a final thought, as it relates to this idea of becoming more like a child. As my own kids have grown, I've noticed that they love to be invited into adventure and that they have a sky-high tolerance for risk. I can say, "Hey, Abram and Callie! Do you want to—" And before I can fill in the blank, two sets of dancing eyes have already said yes.

"Do you want to go camping and see if we can find any bears, even though if we're successful we could get eaten alive?"

"Yes!"

"Do you want to play touch football in the snow, even though it's so cold outside that your noses could freeze and fall right off?"

"Yes!"

"Do you want to see who can eat the most donuts in five minutes flat, even though you might have a bellyache for three days?"

"Yes!"

It has never mattered what the offer is; if it involves adventure and a measure of risk, my kids have always been game. Still, what I want my kids to dive into more than anything is the idea that following Jesus is the best adventure they can have.

Depending on which research survey you read, somewhere between 50–80 percent of today's young adults are turning their backs on the church. These are kids who have been raised in the church, who have been leaders in their youth groups, who have said they want to trust God with their lives. But as soon as they hit age eighteen, they flee church and never come back.

And honestly, I don't blame them a bit.

As older, wiser, more mature Christ followers, we have watered down Jesus' call on our lives and presented a gospel that requires zero risk. Kids look at the Christianity we have created and say, "Why would I give everything to something that costs me nothing?" Instinctively they have surmised that life without risk requires no faith at all. And life without risk is no fun.

And so, in an attempt to inject necessary risk into their lives, they veer off the narrow road and experiment with drugs and booze and sex. They cut themselves with sharp objects just to feel something, just to prove they're really alive. And all the while, Jesus says, "If real life is what you're after, boy, have I got a mission for you."

Certainly, I'm not encouraging senseless risk taking here. (Although when I was a kid, I slept in a bed covered in lead paint, I drank out of a rusty water hose every summer day, I rode around in the back of a pickup truck—with the tailgate down, no less—and I lived to tell about it all.) What I *am* suggesting is that we call out our kids' sense of adventure and point them to Christ, who can lead them on the biggest adventure of their lives. I'm suggesting that we live in such a way that we present a gospel that is risky and raw, and that we show our children by our example that faith is *essential* to the life we live.

In doing so, we grow down, not up. We become the kids Jesus' kingdom is for.

33

JESUS LOVES ME, THIS I KNOW

In April 1992, a young man named Christopher McCandless hiked into the Alaskan wilderness, never to hike out again. For years he had been dreaming of such an adventure, a way to find himself at last. And so, at age twenty-four, armed with only a bag of rice, a few books, several pieces of camping equipment, a box of ammunition, and a gun, he began the hundred-day odyssey that ultimately would claim his life.

McCandless grew up in California, the older of two kids born to a mother who was having an affair with a married man. That man eventually divorced his wife and left his family, which included six kids, to marry Christopher's mom, but the new union would prove equally fragile. McCandless remembered his parents' frequent fights. With a father working for NASA and a mom who was a professional as well, money was never a problem. It was unity that was lacking for them. And it was against this fragmented backdrop that Christopher — their only son — decided to set off for the woods.

In January 1993, *Outside* magazine published a feature article about Chris's life and his untimely death by starvation. The story was later turned into a book that was a bestseller around the globe. Then it became a movie. Millions of people were drawn to the story of the boy who ventured ill-prepared into the wild. I read the account and found it interesting that someone was willing to go to such lengths to find something that was right in front of him all along. We "find ourselves" not in the wilderness but in the unconditional love of Christ.

✦⁓✦

When I was a kid, my parents dragged my siblings and me to Sunday school every weekend, rain or shine. And if there is one song I remember from those obligatory visits, it's the simplest one in the book:

> *Jesus loves me! this I know,*
> *For the Bible tells me so;*
> *Little ones to him belong,*
> *They are weak but he is strong.*
> *Yes, Jesus loves me!*
> *Yes, Jesus loves me!*
> *Yes, Jesus loves me!*
> *The Bible tells me so.*

Maybe I was just a gullible kid, but I actually *believed* those words. I believed that Jesus was strong and loving and that with him I had a place to belong. I sang those words with great passion, because I believed they were true.

You may have too.

But then, like me, you probably experienced a few failures here, a handful of letdowns there, a string of loneliness or sinfulness or darkness or pain. Before you knew it, the belief had faded, a yellowed picture now barely in view. Over time, you brushed up against one too many "I love you's" that panned out to be absolute frauds, and perhaps without intending to, you slowly began to mistrust God, determining he must be fraudulent as well.

But here is a certainty you can bank on: God simply cannot lie. When he says, "I love you," he means it. He can't *not* tell the truth.

+⚇+

Twenty-plus years ago Pam and I had been dating about six months, and we decided to go to church together one Sunday evening and then grab a bite to eat. Pam was driving me home after dinner, and as we were sitting in the driveway of my house, I felt a giant lump form in my throat. There was something I needed to tell her, something I had never told her before.

I hemmed and hawed and fidgeted for a while but then mustered the courage to speak. Taking her hands in mine, I caught her eye and said, "I love you, Pam."

As I gazed into her eyes and squeezed her hands, I anticipated her "I love you too!" But the shape of her mouth was all wrong for those words. Something else entirely was making its way out. "That's great!" she said, with her typical smile. And in two words flat, my heart fell to my feet.

That's *great?*

That's great?!

As I absorbed the full brunt of her words, I thought, *Can't you just lie a little and tell me you love me too?*

I daresay my wife has not told a lie once in her entire life. True to form, she wasn't about to proclaim her love for me if she didn't feel it deep in her bones. And really, what did I know of love? I had been dating her all of six months. We were still two full years from becoming man and wife — so maybe I did jump the gun.

But God? He *never* speaks out of turn. He always means exactly what he says. Truth is his person, his invention, his nature. He cannot and will not lie.

I have wondered from time to time what might have become of Christopher McCandless had he ever fully embraced this truth.

He was a brilliant, inventive, and talented young man who, undeniably, died far too soon. May those of us who have consumed the
richness of God's love never forget the ones walking this planet in
search of a single bite.

⚇

There's a bumper sticker I frequently see around town that says,
"Not all who wander are lost." It's a true statement, but it's also true
that some who wander *are*. And some of those wanderers need the
truth of God's love, if they ever hope to truly find themselves—
and find their way home.

For the record, God does in fact love us. The Bible tells us so.

PART THREE

CARRIERS OF GRACE

*Remembering the grace that embraced us, we
stretch out arms of rescue now.
Leaning, loving, listening, learning — every gracious act
a signpost pointing men and women home.*

34

ROOM FOR BOTH
YOU AND YOUR BURDEN

A young man sits atop his cart and steers his donkey along the road. He is traveling through the countryside, making the familiar trek into town to deliver his handmade goods, when he rounds a curve and finds an elderly man shuffling down the side of the path. The man ambles along, slowly, laboriously, weighed down by the sizable load on his back. The young man pulls up beside him and says, "You're welcome to ride in my cart. I'll see to it you make it into town."

The elderly man exhales, grateful for the lift. He climbs gingerly into the back of the cart and settles into his seat. The young man then urges the donkey toward town.

Half a mile down the road, the young man steals a glance at his traveling companion, wanting to be sure he is faring well, and notices that the man still has his heavy bag positioned on his aching back. He does a double take, disbelieving his own eyes, then chuckles slightly.

"Sir," he says, "the cart is for both you *and* your burden."[16]

✦✧✦

I imagine God did countless double takes during my first decade as a follower of his. We'd be cruising down the road, when he would glance at me, then glance again, saying, *I've got it, Brady, I promise. You can lay your burden down.* If there is one message Christ followers need to hear today, it is that God's cart can carry their load too. "My yoke is easy," Jesus promised us, "and my burden is *light*" (Matt. 11:30).

I get why we doubt this message, that with Christ, life can feel light. All around us, things feel so heavy, so dispiriting and difficult and dark. We've somehow convinced ourselves that there are extra points in heaven for people who just bear up under the load. We struggle and suffer and slug it out, as grace chuckles and shakes its head.

✢⛬✢

During his earthly ministry, Jesus extended a profound offer to his disciples — and to us. "Come to me, all you who are weary and burdened," he said, "and I will give you rest" (Matt. 11:28). When our burden overwhelms us, we can climb into his cart and be relieved. We have met our burden lifter, and he is capable and he is kind. This is *very* good news. We can take a load off as we travel this road called life, and invite others to do the same. And how it changes the tenor of an average day when I invest myself in unburdening the people whose path I happen to cross.

To the man wrapped in the merciless tendrils of online porn and all its wiles: "Heave the burden off your shoulders. Relief is finally yours."

To the woman torn between work and home: "Your burden has been lifted. Trust your Father to lead the way."

To the couple suffocating under a mound of unpaid bills: "Climb into the big-enough cart of God. The ride is perfectly free."

Carriers of grace walk through their day unloading burdens left and right. They invite the mom of three screaming toddlers to slip in front of them in the line at the grocery store. They cover the cost of a cup of coffee and invest a half hour in the homeless man sitting dejected on the street. They lend a careful ear and an open heart to the friend needing a place to vent. They look the clerk at Walmart in the eye and mean it when they ask, "How's it going today?" They train their gaze on the lives around them instead of using up all their energy on themselves.

Where are the burdened ones, they ask, *who may need a lift today?*

35

A BIG OL' SLOPPY HELPING
OF GRACE

My buddy Garvin is as good a friend as a guy could want. He and I met in Amarillo and did ministry together in Texas, and as soon as it was decided that Pam and I would be relocating to Colorado Springs, I knew that if there was one man I wanted working by my side in my new role, it was Garvin McCarrell, hands down. Garvin is the kind of friend who has my permission to say anything to me at any time regarding anything he observes in my life. And the great thing about Garvin is that he does. If I sin in front of Garvin, he will not ignore it. In fact, our history proves that rather than turn a blind eye, he will faithfully bust my chops.

Recently we were in a senior staff meeting together, and at one point during the discussion I came on a little too strong. I knew as soon as the comment left my lips that it probably wasn't the right thing to say. Or the right way to say it. The staff member I had directed my "strength" toward kind of shut down from then on. The meeting dismissed, and en route back to my office, I sensed Garvin's sure presence by my side.

"Hmm ..." That's all he said. I knew what was coming next, so I decided to beat him to the punch.

"I got a little amped up in there," I admitted.

"Yeah," Garvin said with a grin. "Not sure what happened just now was exactly the effect you were going for."

I stopped in the middle of the hallway, told Garvin I would go and make things right, and did an about-face and headed toward the wounded staffer's office.

Five minutes later all was well relationally once more, and I dropped Garvin a quick email telling him thanks. He hadn't incriminated me or indicted me. He hadn't judged me or condemned me. He had simply brought to my attention an opportunity to grow and to be wise. And he did so with *graciousness*, a trait he has always worn very well.

⚔

Tucked deep in the origin of the word *gracious* is the idea that divine revelation has affected your heart so significantly that it now influences your thoughts, your words, and your deeds. Graciousness is when heaven penetrates earth, courtesy of the actions of a daughter or son. It is being kind and loving and gentle even when the person you are dealing with deserves anger or ridicule or scorn. I pray I'm becoming a more gracious person. I'm not perfect in this area, but I am committed to this course.

Where I come from, suppertime could be an Olympic sport. We are serious about food in the South, especially items served in vats as opposed to some dainty china bowl. Take barbecue, for instance. In my hometown, the preferred way to present saucy pulled pork is to lay it out on aluminum garbage can lids. Come on now, admit it—is there anything better than that?

My buddies and I would tromp through the buffet-style line, then sit down at an old picnic table to eat. Once we had downed that first portion, we would head back for a second big ol' sloppy helping of meat. Maybe things could use a little refinement in northwest Louisiana, but this much I am sure of: those people know how to *eat*.

The longer I walk with Christ, and the more people I encounter along the way, the more I find myself applying my hometown eating style to the spiritual realm. These days, I actually *look* for ways to dish up big ol' sloppy helpings of grace.

Let me give you an example. Frequently I am asked by members of the media and people in the community what I think about one hot topic or another. Do I believe abortion is always wrong? Do I think Christ followers can also be gay? Do I support political positions that further distance God from our everyday life?

I can't tell you how liberating it has been to let the Bible answer for me. It doesn't matter what Brady Boyd thinks about an issue; the perspective we should concern ourselves with is *God's*. My view is the Bible's view. So I typically respond to hot-topic questions with themes from a careful examination of what the Bible says. But it's not merely what I say that matters; it's also how I choose to say it. I don't have to be mean about communicating truth. I don't have to yell. I don't have to get defensive. I don't have to wag a pious finger and condemn people for how they choose to live.

Whether they look different or smell different or act different or vote different, I can choose being gracious over being mean. I can love them. I can engage with them. I can seek to be their friend. I can see them the way my Father sees them. Every day, I can be a person of grace.

Yes, we are to champion truth, speak truth, spread the truth all around. I'm just advocating we do so with a big ol' sloppy helping of grace.

✦✼✦

If you have kids, then you know that pharmacies now offer a vast array of delicious flavors to help certain medicines go down easier. Medicine manufacturers finally discovered what parents have long known, which is that the only remedy that can make kids feel better is the remedy that doesn't first get refused. I can still taste the cough syrup I was forced to take as a kid. Tuna fish topped with ketchup—that's about as appealing as things got. But today there is banana and strawberry and cherry and mango and grape. Who wouldn't want a little cough now and then, with flavors like those?

My point is that our world is in dire need of God's good medicine, administered by his sons and daughters. But people rarely digest truth unless it has first been flavored with grace. Full of truth *and* full of grace—this is who we are called to be.

God won us over not with indictment but with grace. Now it's our turn to follow suit.

36

UNTANGLED

Back when the charismatic movement was starting to gain steam, Pam and I were part of a church that had a very excitable worship team. Several singers would lead the congregation in worship for the first twenty or thirty minutes of the service, and one singer in particular would rev up as soon as the first song started. Within fifteen seconds he would be jumping to the beat as if he had mounted a pogo stick. Wireless microphones weren't in vogue yet, and with six or seven singers onstage every Sunday, the platform was a thick web of cords. This young man — the one I couldn't help but watch, even though I was supposed to be reverently worshiping God — would jump and jump and jump, and then, when he *really* got into the music, he would also start to spin and spin and spin. By the second verse, he'd have crafted a straitjacket of cords for himself and would be so entangled that he would have to spend the rest of the song trying inconspicuously to jump and spin the other way.

That memory came to mind recently, and I couldn't help but smile at the image of that bound-up guy. In a way, I relate to him. I have lived tangled up myself.

There was a time in my life when I was so wrapped up in

myself—my needs, my wants, my dreams, my will—that I had no capacity for tending to anyone else. Truly, if there is one thing that keeps otherwise good people from living as selfless carriers of grace, it's that we're too tangled up in the cords of this world to focus our attention on God. We don't see the needs he sees. We don't hear the cries he hears. We don't taste the suffering of so many people in our own backyard who need help.

Every day, millions of Christ followers wake up, start their day, and immediately start to spin. Between their jobs, their families, their to-do lists, their mortgage payments, their social obligations, and the innumerable technology devices that usurp every discretionary moment in their day, they couldn't train their gaze on God if they tried. They want to be still and draw near and lean in and look up and join God in his kingdom work, but they don't know where to begin in getting untangled from all those cords.

✕

I have a friend named Tom who lives as untangled as anyone I know. He looks more like Jesus every time I see him, and after knowing him as long as I've known him, finally I think I know the reason why. The guy *refuses* to let himself get bound by the cares and concerns of this world. He insists on learning more about God each day and then *practices* the new knowledge he's gained. Grace flows in and grace pours out. We need far more Toms in this world.

I have been rereading the book of Luke these last few weeks in preparation for a series at church, and whenever I get to a particular part in chapter 9, I can't help but think of Tom. Verses 23–25 read, "He [Jesus] said to them all [the disciples]: 'Whoever wants to be my disciple must deny themselves and take up their cross daily and follow me. For whoever wants to save their life will lose it, but whoever loses their life for me will save it. What good is it for someone to gain the whole world, and yet lose or forfeit their very self?' "

Daily followership. Living to give, not to gain. An emphasis on caring for one's soul. This is what Jesus was encouraging that day. This is what Tom does so well, and I want to live a little more like Tom. Truth be told, you probably do too.

And so we begin the process of untangling ourselves, one loop at a time. We put down the smartphone, we turn off the radio, we exhale the concerns of the day. We press in to God's ever-near presence and ask, "What are you up to here, now?" We resurrender our plans, our fears, our questions, and our will to our Father's capable hands, and we ask him for the umpteenth time to help us live as freed-up daughters and sons.

37

FIRST,
A HEART OF COMPASSION

A woman happened upon New Life's campus who was incoherent and scared. A member of our staff named Melody found her roaming aimlessly across our grounds, and as the mysterious woman's story tumbled out in sentence fragments and nonsensical words, we pieced together that she wasn't from around here, but we couldn't pinpoint where she was from; that her credit cards had been stolen, but she couldn't remember how; and that she needed desperately to get home, but she couldn't put her finger on why.

Melody assured the woman she was in good hands, she led her to our prayer center, she set her up in a prayer room with something to eat and something to drink, and then she excused herself briefly so she could sort out what to do next. After googling the woman's name, she was elated to find a blog entry from a family in Virginia that was pleading with the world at large to provide any information possible on their mom's/sister's/daughter's whereabouts. The lady had been missing for what felt to them like a very long time—ten days, maybe?—and nobody knew where she was. What's more, according to the blog, she suffered from mental illness and would require "an extra measure of compassion if she was ever to find her way home."

Our staff member placed a call to the family and told them their loved one was safe and sound. A day later they were all reunited; one who had been lost was joyfully found.

＊☙＊

I have never been around such a compassionate group of people as those I've found at New Life Church. They love to give, they love to serve, they love to consider others' needs ahead of their own. But it's not just their behavior that impresses me; it's the posture of their *hearts*.

Compassion is an inside-out work, a bubbling up of what's already happening in a person's inner world. Compassion says, "I'm not going to overlook you, judge you, or cast you aside when you're so obviously in need. I'm here to be helpful, whatever that looks like, and however long it takes." And what strikes me about the most compassionate folks I know is that their hearts respond long before their hands.

I've been trying to pay attention to this dynamic in my own life in an effort to discern whether I'm really as compassionate as I tend to think I am. Which brings me to last month.

I was sitting in the basement of our home, catching up on the national news. As I stared at the TV, I saw images scroll one after the other, each depicting worse and worse forms of devastation in the aftermath of a major weather event. "Thunderstorms, severe winds, and tornadoes slammed the South on Wednesday," the news anchor said, "killing dozens of people in four states."

I saw houses whose roofs were the only thing visible because floodwaters had risen so high. Entire farms had been swept away, along with the acres of crops they had planted just weeks before. I watched as men and women walked like zombies down neighborhood streets, pointing at the foundations that once held up their homes, and all I could think was, *This is not just news footage to me.*

Real families made up of real moms and dads with hopes and

dreams for the kind of life their kids will enjoy, and real kids eager to enjoy those dreams—these were the lives being affected. These were the people in need. I watched them watching what was left of their lives float by, and I thought, *What on earth would I do?* I have cherished belongings in our home, things my dad left me before he died, family photos I could never replace, loved ones' letters that are significant to me. I couldn't imagine how those families would begin to rebuild their devastated lives.

As I sat there dumbstruck on my couch—in my house that was still standing, where everything inside was safe and secure—I said aloud, "God, have mercy on these people. Please, surround them with your love." It was a reaction that wouldn't have been true of me in the years before I surrendered to Christ. He has graciously carved compassion into my heart so that I can respond appropriately to people in pain. Sure, I still have to beat down cynicism from time to time, to keep it from having its way. But with ever-increasing frequency, I sense the compassion of God standing its ground in my mind and my heart.

✦❈✦

Matthew 20 tells the story of two blind men receiving sight. Jesus and his disciples were leaving the town of Jericho and happened upon men sitting on the side of the road. A large crowd was flanking Jesus, as usual, and as the blind men heard the throng approaching, they yelled, "Lord, Son of David, have mercy on us!" (v. 30).

The crowd surrounding Jesus told the men to pipe down. Evidently, they didn't think the Messiah wanted his very important business interrupted by a couple of screamers who couldn't see. The screamers didn't comply. "Lord, Son of David!" they shouted louder still. "Have mercy on us!" (v. 31).

I envision the scene then falling perfectly silent as Jesus stopped walking and turned toward those men. "What do you want me to do for you?" he asked, to which the men said, "We want our sight" (vv. 32–33).

Jesus' heart of compassion took over. How could he *not* meet that need? He walked over to where they sat, he reached out and touched their eyes, and immediately they were healed. The text says they then "followed him" (v. 34).

And it's understandable that they did, right?

If there is one thing our compassionate response offers the world, it is the chance to see life like never before. Compassion extended in the name of Christ opens eyes, heals wounds, ushers the kingdom of heaven onto planet Earth. Jesus knew that his model of compassion would spur us on to live life like that too. He knew that when we were tempted to grow bitter and cynical, we would slow our pace, look at his example, and preserve the goodness that still dwells in our brave hearts.

He knew that when we encountered wayward women who don't know how to find their way home, or when we saw entire counties of people rendered homeless from treacherous storms, or when we were interrupted during our day's activities by someone shouting a request for our help—he knew that in these instances and a thousand others, we would act on what we feel deep inside. We would act from a compassionate heart.

38

SEEING OTHERS
FOR WHO THEY ARE

The first gift I ever gave to my son, Abram, I gave to him when he was three weeks old. It was a blue-and-white baseball cap, and I still remember looking at him with that tiny cap perched atop his head, thinking how much fun we'd have when he was old enough to play catch. I also bought him a miniature baseball glove, which I would position just beside his infant seat, as though broadcasting to the watching world, "My son is *destined* to be an athlete."

But then Abram began to grow up. Two, three, four years old, and still he had no interest in throwing a ball with Dad. I would urge him out to the backyard, stick that glove on his small hand, stand him a few feet from me, and toss him the ball. Time and again, the ball would land on the grass beside him. Toss, plop. Toss, plop. Toss, plop. He didn't even pretend to enjoy the game I just knew he'd love.

When Abram turned five, I decided that what he needed was the camaraderie of a T-ball team. Naturally, I was one of the coaches for his team, and I distinctly remember watching Abram stand absentmindedly in the outfield, counting the minutes until the practice or the game was over. He would engage anyone within shouting distance in a conversation about the intricate structures that could be built with Legos, while the ball rolled right by his planted feet. Other kids would race to nab a fly ball, but not Abram. He would eye the soaring ball with a half-dazed glance and then return his attention to whatever string of creative thoughts had captured his imagination.

What was obvious to everyone else was the one thing I refused to admit: Abram Boyd is many great things, but *athlete* is not one of them. He has a brilliant engineering mind that he got from his biological dad, and while he has deep interest in knowing how things work and in dreaming up ways to make them better, sports just aren't his thing.

Still, despite Abram's apathy toward baseball, I wouldn't let him quit the team. We had made a commitment to play for one season, and I felt strongly that he should finish what he started. Plus, it wasn't *all* bad for Abram. He enjoyed wearing the striped uniform with the number on the back, for example. And he looked forward to postgame snacks. As long as food was involved, he showed up to play. But his interest in the sport never grew.

As a former athlete, I felt dejected and sad, but the emotions I experienced as Abram's dad sang to a far different tune. Somehow I sensed God telling me that he had everything under control. *Brady, I placed specific gifts in Abram,* he would say. *Your job is not to wish I'd planted different gifts. Your job is to draw out the ones that are there.*

Abram was in the second grade before I fully grasped what God was saying, thanks to a run-of-the-mill parent-teacher conference on an otherwise typical Tuesday night.

On the appointed evening, Pam and I went to Abram's school, and as we folded ourselves into two miniature desk chairs and looked up at Abram's teacher, who was sitting in a "big-people" seat, I braced for the worst. I already knew that Abram had been struggling socially — the teacher had told us as much along the way — and I wondered what other bad news would be delivered to me now.

The teacher looked at me and said, "You know, I have a nephew a lot like Abram."

She eyed Pam and then me—one part kindness, one part pity—and then continued. "Let me give you a few of my thoughts." Another agonizing pause. Then finally: "Mr. and Mrs. Boyd, the worst thing you could do to Abram is to try to change him into someone he is not. Let your son be who he is. It's kids such as Abram who grow up and invent things that change the world, because they see things ... differently ... than anyone else."

And there it was: our kid was *different*. Surely that couldn't be good.

I hadn't especially liked this teacher. She had always struck me as loud and brash and a bit too liberal in her approach. But when those words came out of her mouth, I knew she had been placed in the Boyd family's path by none other than God himself. The wisdom she imparted to Pam and me that day altered our course with our son. For my part, I began to see Abram as a world changer, instead of as the kid who had doused my dreams.

Not long after that meeting, I received a word of encouragement from God that affirmed what Abram's teacher had said: *Abram is going to invent something someday, Brady, and it will in fact change the world.*

The prompting was so strong, so clear, that I decided to tell Abram what I had heard. He responded neutrally—a subtle nod, something of a shoulder shrug—which made me wonder if he understood what I had said. A full six years would pass before I would come to see how impactful my words had been.

✦⚬✦

Several weeks ago Abram, now thirteen, and I attended something our church calls Guys' Night Out, this one involving the fantastic combination of Bible teaching and a chili cook-off. Soon after we arrived, Abram noticed that his nose was bleeding. I was supposed to take the stage to speak to a roomful of men, so one of the guys in our congregation offered to accompany Abram to a bathroom and help him clean up his face. Later that man told me that he and Abram had struck up a conversation while they waited for his nose to quit bleeding, and that Abram talked about what he wanted to be when he grew up. "Brady," the guy said, "did you know your son wants to be an inventor? He says he is going to invent something someday that will change the world!"

Back in the bathroom, the man had quipped that maybe Abram could invent some sort of postal-sorting system that would automatically shove mail through everyone's front door, not unlike the process seen in the first Harry Potter movie. Without missing a beat, Abram replied, "Sir, I said I'd invent something that will *change the world.* Not something as trivial as *that.*"

Ah, my boy was finally catching it. He was starting to believe what both his heavenly Father and his earthly dad believe about him, that his uncommon mind will be used in a colossal way at some point in his life.

When someone sees the potential our heavenly Father has placed in another and then works to draw it out, young men begin to live as sons and young women to live as daughters. An entire destiny can be altered with a single divinely inspired, well-placed word.

❦

When I was thirty years old, I had no idea I had the gift of prophecy. I was pastoring a tiny church in Hereford, Texas, and after a worship service, I was standing at the altar to meet with anyone in need of prayer. A friend of mine, who pastored another church, was in town that weekend helping me lead the service, and as he and I stood side by side to pray over one woman in particular, I received what I believed to be a word from God for her. In the middle of my prayer, I spoke the word of encouragement the Lord had given me, and then I closed the prayer. As I looked up, I saw tears streaming down her cheeks. "You have no way of knowing this," she said, "but what you said just then ... that is *exactly* what I needed to hear."

My friend and I went on about our day, ministering to people in need. Then, over lunch, he said, "Brady, I never knew your gift of prophecy was so vibrant and so strong."

I had never considered myself the prophetic type, but after hearing this guy rattle off example after example of my gift in action from the weekend we had just experienced, I was intrigued. Looking back, I see how that single comment awakened something deep inside me and launched me into an entirely new field of ministry, opening my eyes to opportunities I never otherwise would have pursued. I studied the gift, I exercised the gift, and now prophetic encouragement is a major part of my ministry.

Here's what I'm learning about people and potential and our role as daughters and sons: When we are more concerned about knowing how God is working in people's lives than we are about changing those people to fit our expectations, the odds are exponentially higher that we will play a part in their potential becoming reality. We can see people as God sees them. We can discover the way that they are wired. We can speak out the potential we find tucked inside.

Purveyor of the *possible*—it's a chief role of the daughter and son.

39

A GUN, A HATCHET, AND A HORSE

When I was nine years old, I had a gun, a hatchet, and a horse—all gifts from my dad. Putting resources like these in the hands of a child might be considered negligence today, but back then it signified a transfer of trust. Dad taught me to use them carefully and to be a good steward of their power, and then he confidently set me free.

During summer months I would be gone all day, by myself or on occasion with my brother, with nothing but those three things at hand. I would ride deep into the woods surrounding our county, splashing through creeks, chasing frogs or fish, stopping only to take aim at a water moccasin slithering by. I would chop down trees and build sky-high forts and shoot at scurrying critters left and right. And not once would my dad worry about his adventure-some son. I knew the places I was allowed to go, and he knew he had trained me well.

I should mention that I didn't always follow the training I had received.

One of the more interesting dynamics of growing up in small-town Louisiana is that your neighbors are related to you somehow.

Everybody is somebody's second cousin twice removed or sister's daughter's nephew, and the net effect on you as a rambunctious kid is that you don't get away with a *thing*. There wasn't a person in our community who didn't have assumed permission to spank me, if they discovered I was acting up. For example, I once started a fire on a "neighbor's" property. Who knew green grass could catch like that? I think I still have a handprint of that particular family member's to show for my ill-advised pyromania.

Today I look back on those events of my childhood with nothing but gratefulness and respect. And now that I'm tasked with creating culture in a leadership role, I try to employ those small-town ideals. Environments welcoming of appropriate boundaries, reasonable discipline, and consistent love are environments marked by trust. That's the kind of place I grew up in; it's the kind of place I choose to live in now.

✼✄✼

A study was once conducted involving school-age children and the school's playground. Day after day, as soon as the recess bell sounded, kids flooded the playground and occupied every square inch of the field. They lined the fences, they ran back and forth across huge swaths of grass, and they perched on monkey bars and swings and seesaws, while chatting, laughing, and screaming their delight for as long as they were allowed to play. But then something drastic changed.

One morning the recess bell rang, and as usual the kids flew through the school's doors. But within minutes, observers noted, every child remained huddled quietly in the center of the field. They were not roaming and playing and laughing and screaming; they seemed anxious and insecure. The only thing different about the playground that day was that the fences had been removed.

It's not just children who crave boundaries; despite our protests to the contrary, we adults appreciate them too. Even the most independent-minded of us would crumble in a world without limits. We want to know where the lines are. We want to feel protected. We want to live in an environment where we consistently know the score. Sure, we may push back or rebel from time to time, but often rebellion is simply a means for clarifying exactly where the boundaries are.

My dad knew well what I have come to learn: a lack of boundaries cannot promote freedom, any more than stupidity can promote good sense. To have—and stay within—appropriate boundaries is to experience what it means to live free.

When I first arrived at New Life, parts of the culture were badly flawed. For example, I quickly discovered that a common belief among our ministry staff was that they were only as important as their proximity to me, the head guy. The net effect was troubling: If I didn't attend a meeting, that meeting was deemed unimportant. If I didn't say something directly to someone, the message was not legitimate. If I didn't drop by various people's offices three times a week, they clearly were not valued or loved.

My first few months on the job, I felt just like Moses, who wound up spending all of his time doing what he should have delegated to others on his team, and nearly went nuts as a result. Some members of our ministry team were so desperate for attention that they would trail me across the parking lot each evening as I was making my way to my car. They would flank me for the two-minute trek and expect me in that short span of time to knock out every decision they needed made. "Can I get a new computer?" "Can we launch this new ministry?" "What do you think of so-and-so for such-and-such a job?"

Eventually Moses's father-in-law, Jethro, talked him into appointing some help, and ultimately that is what I also did to fight my way back to sane. I told the staff that I loved them and that I was committed to leading them well but that I would rely on a *team* of trusted senior leaders to help me get that done. I reminded them of our organizational chart, which reflected direct supervisors for all. "If you'd like to talk about your personal growth, your family's goings-on, or what God is up to in your life, I'm the guy to chase down. But for *management* issues, you go to your *manager*. That's why they are given that name. You will receive better attention and more thoughtful decisions by approaching them, as opposed to hurling curveballs my way at the end of a day and expecting instantaneous results."

It would have been impulsive of me to tackle weighty issues during those two-minute parking-lot forums, and impulsivity in a leader is the mark of an orphan, not a son. I refuse to operate that way.

It took some time—and some false starts—to clean up our protocol. But as the weeks wore on, our boundaries came into view, and all of us were healthier as a result.

✵

Another challenge facing me in my early days at the church centered on establishing discipline as part of our cultural grid. One of the first trends I had to correct upon my arrival at my new post was the staff's abuse of time. I couldn't look inside any ministry department without finding a workaholic or two. Performance had been rewarded previously, and performers many of them were.

I pulled the staff together and explained that a new leadership day had dawned, in which *productivity*, not performance, would be prized. I told them that they were to be away from home no more than three nights a week and that under no circumstances should anybody be working more than fifty hours a week. I knew there would be periodic exceptions to the rule, but I asked the staff to make those rare. "There are thousands of churches around the world that will let you work yourself into burnout," I said. "But New Life is not among them."

Additionally, I met with staff members' spouses and told them eyeball to eyeball that they had my complete permission — even my *encouragement* — to call me directly if their ministry-loving spouses violated these new rules. Over the ensuing months, a few took me up on the offer. The subsequent meetings with their spouses were always short and sweet. "Nobody will be allowed to sacrifice family for the sake of ministry," I'd remind them. "And 'nobody' happens to include you." They would just look at me and nod.

The church can become a mistress if we are not diligent about keeping each other in check. This is the power of reasonable discipline in an environment marked by trust. God disciplines people he loves, "as a father the son he delights in" (Prov. 3:12). If I want to maintain my role as a spiritual father, I have no choice but to follow suit.

✦✖✦

If there was a third category that had to be addressed in order to develop a trust-fueled place, it was love — unconditional, appropriate, healthy love, love that reflects God himself. My practices here were painfully simple: be knowable and be known, be predictable and be pure, be consistent from hour to hour and also from year to year. The caution for a senior ministry leader is the same as for a leader of any organization, community, or group: Whatever you do, don't damage the formation of people you are leading. God is at work in all the world; therefore he is at work in the lives of those we lead. The worst thing we could do as leaders would be to hamper the progress being made. The best thing we could do, however, would be to respond with gratitude to God's lavish love and look to extend that love to those we lead — for leaders love well.

Several years ago a parenting book came out that encouraged moms and dads to see their kids through the lens of God's tenderness toward those children and to raise them accordingly. The author contended that only by seeing our sons and daughters as God himself sees them will we raise morally strong and spiritually motivated children. I find his approach worthwhile not only for physical parents but for spiritual parents as well.

Grace-Based Parenting, the book is called, and in it Dr. Tim Kimmel suggests that if we want to show our kids how to find love, purpose, and hope in Jesus Christ, we should promote an environment in which four freedoms are valued and encouraged: the freedom to be different, the freedom to be vulnerable, the freedom to be candid, and the freedom to make mistakes.[17]

In my view, it's simply another path toward that trust-fueled environment I am committed to fostering. "You are free to be different," we can tell people we lead. "You are free to be vulnerable too. This is a place where you can be candid without fearing retribution, and where you can fail without getting kicked to the curb." We can teach our teams to be good stewards of these liberties and then confidently set them free.

40

MY KNOBBY-KNEED
PEACH FESTIVAL GIRL

The year was 1975, and my bride, Pam, was a knobby-kneed six-year-old living in Ruston, Louisiana. As was the annual tradition for young girls in her town, on the appointed day, she put on her best dress and her most charming smile, and she vied for the title Miss Princess Peach. It was a beauty pageant, plain and simple, and not surprisingly, Pam did well. Which would have been meaningless to my wife, except for the exciting ride in a convertible she would then get to take as a star in the Peach Festival parade. Big stuff for a small-town girl.

Since the day Pam and I said, "I do," I have kept a framed photograph of the six-year-old version of my bride posing in that Miss Princess Peach dress on a bookshelf in my office—not to commemorate her pageant participation but to remind me that the woman I am married to was once someone's little girl.

Pam is all woman—winsome, mature, strong, smart, and sure—and yet just below the surface still resides a fragile soul. The kid who once sported those cascading curls, that ruffled dress, and those long, birdlike legs still needs thoughtful attention, a gentle touch, conversation, commitment, and care. Men succeed as husbands only when they call "daughter" forth from their wives; our women are prized creations of a loving but jealous God.

✢⚯✢

Pastoral ministry lends itself to a fair amount of marriage counseling, and on a near-weekly basis I find myself sitting across from a husband whose marriage is in dire straits. Invariably, the discussion winds up focusing on one simple misstep toward marital bliss: somewhere along the way, the guy fails to acknowledge day in and day out that he is wed to a daughter of the King. "If you are mistreating your wife or withholding your care," I explain, "if you are neglecting to lead her well, remember that you are doing these things to a girl who is the apple of her Daddy's eye. It matters to God how his daughters are treated. It needs to matter to guys like us too." I show them the small, yellowed photo of my Princess Peach and ask them to reconsider their ways.

Granted, sometimes the wife really is the primary cause of the couple's struggle and strife. But more often than not, I find that when the husband is reminded of this fundamental truth, the marriage gets unstuck. Eyes are opened, hearts are tenderized, fists become unclenched, postures relax. Sighs of resolution are exhaled, God-honoring determination is fixed, steps of progress are taken, and broken covenants—thankfully—are put back together again.

✢⚯✢

Tucked deep inside every man's wife is a wide-eyed six-year-old with a thousand questions on her mind: *Do you see me? Do you value me? Do you know me? Do you care? Do you delight in my presence? Do you miss me when I'm not around?* By our words and by our actions, we as their husbands can offer a resounding yes. What a noble role we have as sons, to love God's daughters well.

One of the dynamics that has helped me learn to love Pam as "daughter" has been fathering a daughter of my own. I often ask men who have daughters to pay closer attention to those pint-size females as a way to get inside their wife's mind and heart. Typically, they eye me with a glazed-over look, as though I'm asking them to spout off the square root of 4,683. But it's true.

For the past decade, I have learned all about the "world of girl," courtesy of one Callie Grace Boyd. I see what lights her up and what shuts her down, what encourages her and what makes her sad. I listen to her hopes, her dreams, her problems, and her fears, and every time, I come away not just a better dad but also a better *husband*. In Callie, I see vulnerabilities and insecurities, the young places that have yet to grow strong, and it somehow informs my understanding of the woman I share a bed with every night.

"Husbands, love your wives," Paul says in Ephesians 5:25, "just as Christ loved the church and gave himself up for her." I want this kind of sacrificial posture to characterize my love for Pam. Not just to bless her life but also to model for our daughter how she should insist on being treated someday. Callie and I have a frequent exchange in our home that goes something like this:

(Me) "Callie, you know you can't marry anybody who doesn't treat you at least as well as Dad treats you, right?"

(Callie) "Ewww, gross! I hate boys and have *no* plans of marrying one, Dad. Ever."

The fact that my daughter has yet to catch boy fever is fine by me. But I know there will come a point when that will shift. And when it does, I want her to share life with a man who knows how to treat a daughter of God.

41

HUMILITY,
AND HOW WE'VE PERFECTED IT

A decade ago I was pastoring at a church in the Dallas–Fort Worth area, and I was part of a leadership team that had strong ties to another church in Texas. One of the greatest joys of those ministry years was the bond that united our two congregations. "Sister churches," we called ourselves, and we aimed to serve each other, pray for each other, and build each other up.

One of the ways we did that was that various pastors from their church would fly to Dallas to speak to our congregation, while many of our pastors would fly across the state to speak to theirs. This went on for many months before I noticed that although many of my colleagues were being invited to go preach during weekend services, no one had invited me. My feelings were hurt. I *knew* these guys. I had invested deeply in their church body. I thought our respect was mutual. Didn't I deserve better than this?

And so the struggle in my soul raged on. I wanted to honor Jesus with my attitude. But I wanted that speaking gig more.

A few more months went by, and my bitterness only grew. Finally, I knew I had to confess my sin before it ate me alive. I called a mentor-friend who was part of our congregation and asked for some time with him to bare my soul.

After recounting the situation over coffee, I said plainly, "I feel like I'm being overlooked." I felt gross admitting it, but it was the truth.

My friend heard my confession without recrimination and told me in essence to go in peace. Which I did. In fact, I left his presence feeling fifty pounds lighter than when I had arrived. Confession really is good for the soul.

⚯

The days following that meeting were what I call clean-hands days. For the first time in months, I felt free from all bitterness, envy, and spite. My conversations with God were enjoyable again, now that I was no longer carrying a grudge. I felt released from the bondage that trips us up when we futilely try to keep score.

And then the phone rang.

Exactly one week after I had confessed my prideful spirit to my friend, I answered a call from the senior pastor of the sister church. "Pastor Brady," he said with cheeriness to spare, "would you do us the honor of speaking here one weekend soon?"

Do them the *honor*? If he had known how petty and self-focused I'd been, he probably would have withdrawn his request.

Here is what I learned during that terrible and terrific experience: It's not beyond God to withhold blessing in my life until I see fit to get my attitude straight. Loving fathers know when to hand over good things and when to hold back until the time is right.

I have recently been hit with this reminder, from the flip side of the fatherly coin.

My son turns fourteen next month, and already he is pleading with me to let him drive. Some delinquent New Lifer must have tipped Abram off, because I guarantee I haven't broached this subject with him. "You can't even get a *permit* for another twelve months!" I explained to my *way*-younger-than-sixteen son, who in response only upped his pitch. Finally, we agreed to a few "practice sessions" for starters. On my riding lawn mower. In the safety of our driveway. With careful supervision.

I realize Abram may not appreciate my approach at the moment, but I'm pacing him because I care about him. I care about his well-being. I care about his development. I care about his eventual success. And because of all that care, I refuse to let a fourteen-year-old get behind the wheel of my four-ton truck. Again, good dads know when to place things in their kids' hands and when to wait.

These days, I'm trying to trust God's judgment as consistently as I expect my son to trust mine. The book of Isaiah says this: "Who among you fears the LORD and obeys the word of his servant? Let the one who walks in the dark, who has no light, trust in the name of the LORD and rely on their God. But now, all you who light fires and provide yourselves with flaming torches, go, walk in the light of your fires and of the torches you have set ablaze. This is what you shall receive from my hand: You will lie down in torment" (Isa. 50:10–11).

Those words nail me every time.

If you and I insist on lighting our own fires—landing our own opportunities, securing our own resources, charting our own course, making a name for ourselves instead of fighting for God's fame alone—we will reap a devastating harvest of insecurity, torment, and pain.

I don't want that to be me. And yet the sway of the world only gets stronger, encouraging us to keep setting our own torches ablaze.

It is estimated that more than 100 million people now use Twitter, the online social networking service where users send brief posts to their network of followers. Just last week I came across a study conducted by Rutgers University about what all the tweeting is about. According to the two professors running the study, eight out of ten users' 200 million daily posts can be categorized as "all about me."

"Eighty percent of regular users are 'meformers' [as opposed to informers], people who use the platform to post updates on their everyday activities, social lives, feelings, thoughts, and emotions," the researchers wrote."[18] Only 20 percent share information not pertaining to themselves.

Eighty percent! The vast majority of messages you and I feel compelled to communicate to our friends center on our favorite subject: *us.*

Listen, I'm as prone as the next guy to using Twitter to tout the greatness of my LSU Tigers or rave about my children's latest accomplishments. But the study made me at least ask the question, If it's true that my words betray my heart, then what does a vehicle such as Twitter prove is most important to me?

God says, "Enough with the self-promotion. Trust *me* to light your fire."

＊ᨦ＊

As I mentioned, I've been giving this topic of humility some thought lately and wondering why it's so hard to be humble. This, of course, makes me think of that old Mac Davis song. When I was growing up, the only types of music we listened to in our home were country, western, and country and western—with an occasional hymn thrown in for good measure. If I close my eyes, I can still hear Mac's voice from a crackly radio filling the cab of Dad's old pickup truck as we bounced along unpaved roads:

Oh, Lord, it's hard to be humble
When you're perfect in every way.
I can't wait to look in the mirror
Cause I get better looking each day.

It's a fun song to belt out, mostly because it is over-the-top obnoxious in a lovably self-focused sort of way. And the lyrics *would* be funny if they didn't hit so close to home. Perhaps without meaning to, you and I and every other living, breathing person out there are veering toward becoming a band of narcissists who really do think life's all about us.

Clearly, this is not what Christ intended as our takeaway when he modeled selflessness and service and grace.

✂

One time Jesus told a story to a group of dinner guests who had gathered in the home of a very religious man. Jesus couldn't help but notice how all of the guests elbowed each other out of the way in hopes of securing the best seat at the table, and he thought that maybe they could use a refresher course on what following him really meant.

"When someone invites you to a wedding feast," he said, "do not take the place of honor, for a person more distinguished than you may have been invited. If so, the host who invited both of you will come and say to you, 'Give this person your seat.' Then, humiliated, you will have to take the least important place. But when you are invited, take the lowest place, so that when your host comes, he will say to you, 'Friend, move up to a better place.' Then you will be honored in the presence of all the other guests. For all those who exalt themselves will be humbled, and those who humble themselves will be exalted" (Luke 14:7–11).

Here's the lesson I am learning, as I attempt to walk humility's path: when I leave my promotion to God instead of insisting on lighting my own torch, something in me actually gets *excited* about letting others enjoy the limelight. Jesus' comment about giving the other person the best seat is easy to follow once your view of yourself has been set right according to the ever-humble example of Christ. Humility, then, is not thinking less of ourselves; it is simply thinking of ourselves less. Daughters and sons of a holy God strike this balance, trusting God with their promotion and setting their sights instead on making sure outsiders are humbly given the best seat.

42

FOR FREEDOM,
WE ARE SET FREE

everal months ago Pam and I met a woman with a pretty dramatic past. From age fourteen to age twenty-nine, she was kept
enslaved by a cult and was used for prostitution to help fund the
cult's activities. The more she described her dark history, the more
sobered I became.

Her abuse involved satanic rituals and frequent drug-induced
comas, which explains how she never knew that in the early days of
her association with the cult, she became pregnant, carried a child
to full term, and delivered—miraculously—a healthy baby girl.
Just before we met, she discovered that she had a daughter who is
now fourteen years old and is being used for prostitution, just as
she had been. Day and night this mom devotes herself to helping
her daughter find the freedom she now enjoys.

Admittedly, there are risks, not the least of which is providing
local authorities with the names and addresses of people who do
not wish to be found. But now that she has tasted real freedom and
has stepped into the family of God, she can't bear for her daughter to be relegated to the life of an orphan. I think it was Mother
Teresa who said that the biggest disease of today's generation is not
leprosy or tuberculosis or AIDS, but rather the feeling of being

deserted by people we love. This mom is finally grasping all that "daughter" really means in her own life, and that newfound, life-altering knowledge compels her to fight to rescue her child.

✦☿✦

For many weeks after I met that woman, her story stuck with me the way a bug hangs on to the windshield. The question that vexed me was this: Am I still so grateful for my spiritual freedom that I'm utterly *compelled* to help set others free? When I see someone in bondage—either of their own accord or otherwise—does the desire to judge them or the desire to graciously show them the way out show up most quickly in me? The apostle Paul said that the reason why you and I have been set free is to promote the cause of freedom wherever we go. Despite lesser motivations that may run through our hearts, the primary reason God has freed us is so that we can then help others get free.

I know what you are probably thinking right now. "If I had a story as intense as that woman's, I'd be that passionate too." You stack your history against that of someone who has known escape from slavery and abuse and find yours strangely lacking in flair. But I doubt that God sees things that way when he looks at your story and mine. It cost his one and only Son *everything* to see people such as us freed.

In his book *24 Hours That Changed the World*, author Adam Hamilton writes, "We are meant to look at the cross and see both God's great love and the costliness of grace and to find our hearts changed by what God has done for us. We are meant, as a result of understanding that cost, to serve God with humble gratitude, and to long, as we see Jesus suffer, never to sin again. And yet, of course, we will sin again and call again upon the grace of God revealed on the cross. Like Barabbas, we walk away free because of the suffering of an innocent man."[19]

The grace of the cross is *costly* grace. We cheapen it when we forget this truth, but, oh, the power of remembering it well.

A New Lifer named Joan was a professional nurse for four decades and, upon retirement, decided to put her proven skills to work by volunteering at the Dream Centers of Colorado Springs, the clinic I mentioned earlier that offers free medical treatment to the underinsured women of our city. In doing so, Joan remembers well the price that Jesus paid so that she can live healthy and free.

A thirty-year-old member of our fellowship, Jeremiah, was raised by a derelict dad but found himself at age fifteen sitting in a church service, where a visiting pastor onstage called him out of the crowd and said, "God is here to be your dad." Instantaneously something was loosed in Jeremiah, who had carried an orphan spirit all his life. From that day on, he became a spiritual father to young men in crisis, pointing them to God, who wants to be the dad they never had. Today he runs a nonprofit ministry that seeks to show spiritual orphans how to find their way home — and every day Jeremiah ministers, he remembers well the cost of grace.

A family in our community who already had their hands full with two young children spent months praying and preparing to adopt a sibling group of three kids out of Colorado's foster care program. "We believe every child deserves to be adopted twice," they said. "First, by a loving family. And second, into the kingdom of God. We are committed to doing everything in our power to give these kids what they deserve." *This* is remembering well the cost of the grace of the cross.

If there is a single request I pray each day, it is that God would remind me of one simple truth: we are freed to help others find freedom. There is no higher calling than that.

43

IN FAVOR OF
INCONVENIENCE

If you followed me around on a typical workday, one conclusion you would quickly come to is that I'm not fond of wasted time. The upside is that I get a lot done in a day; the downside is that interruptions make me cringe. This frequently causes me to ask myself, *Why is this frustrating me so deeply? It's not like people are trying to ruin my day.*

If you're a schedule keeper like me, you will totally understand what I am about to say: If people could just schedule their interruptions with me, I would tend to those interruptions with flawless grace. It's just that they are *not* on my schedule. And only what's on my schedule gets done. I plan my work, and I work my plan — is there anything so bad about that?

You probably know the story of the good Samaritan (Luke 10:25–37) by heart, but just to be sure we are on the same page: One day, Jesus was approached by an Old Testament scholar who was trying to trip up the Messiah. The scholar hoped to trap Jesus in his own logic and thereby cripple his credibility in front of a crowd.

"Teacher," he asked Jesus, "what must I do to inherit eternal life?" Of course, being an expert in Levitical law, the man already knew the answer. Jesus evidently didn't appreciate being sassed by the guy, so he threw the ball back in his court. "How do you read it?" Jesus replied, to which the expert in the law said, " 'Love the Lord your God with all your heart and with all your soul and with all your strength and with all your mind'; and, 'Love your neighbor as yourself.' "

"You have answered correctly," Jesus said. "Do this and you will live."

But the scholar wasn't ready to admit defeat. He piped up yet again. "And who is my neighbor?"

Jesus answered the man with a story he trusted would get his point across.

"A man was going down from Jerusalem to Jericho," Jesus said, "when he was attacked by robbers. They stripped him of his clothes, beat him and went away, leaving him half dead. A priest happened to be going down the same road. He was a holy man, a man who was to represent God better than anyone else. But instead of stopping to help the man, he passed by on the other side.

"Later," Jesus continued, "a Levite happened by. Like you, he was an expert in the Scriptures and represented the holiest of holy people. He saw the man left for dead in the ditch. But he too passed by.

"Finally, a Samaritan came upon the man while traveling the very same road. But instead of passing by, the Samaritan stopped, knelt beside the anguished man, bandaged his wounds, loaded him onto his donkey, and rode with him to a nearby inn. There he instructed the innkeeper to care for the ailing man's needs and to keep a tally of any expenses incurred. 'I'll be back again in a few days,' said the Samaritan, 'and will reimburse you the full amount.' "

Looking at the scholar, Jesus said, "Which of these three do you think was a neighbor to the man who fell into the hands of robbers?"

The expert in the law replied, "The one who had mercy on him."

"Go and do likewise," Jesus said. "Anyone you find in need? *That* person is your neighbor."[20]

❤

Now, although the biblical text doesn't delve into this particular detail, one thing that *must* have been true for the hypothetical Samaritan in Jesus' tale was that he didn't wake that morning expecting to find a half-dead man in a ditch along the path. The type A part of my personality wonders if, when he stumbled upon the man in need, the Good Samaritan might even have had a few bad thoughts creep in. Maybe it's just me—most likely, it *is* just me—but on a not-so-infrequent basis, my inner monologue upon finding a person in need goes something like this: *Am I going to stick to my schedule here, or am I going to scrap my plans and follow through on being neighborly today?*

Here's where people who are sold-out followers of Christ are separated from his mere fans: followers are willing to be inconvenienced in order to be Jesus to someone they meet. As I have admitted, I really struggle on this front. But by God's grace, I'm coming around.

❤

Recently I received an email from a friend who runs a rescue mission here in town. His note said that things were reaching desperate status. "We're having to cut back on the amount of food we give to families," he said, "because the pantry is nearly bare." Real kids with real hunger were not being fed in our town, while I pulled up my chair to a juicy hamburger and fries, with a pantry full of options back at home. Several of New Life's pastors and I met and decided to alert our entire congregation to the need and invite them to restock the food pantry that week.

Saturday morning dawned, and as is customary around the Boyd house, I woke ready to take one of my kids to breakfast, just the two of us. This time it was Abram's turn, and en route to the diner, I said, "Abram, we are going to do things a little differently today. We're going to eat breakfast like we always do, but afterward you and I are going shopping."

I had set aside a sum of money that Pam and I agreed to use in helping feed those families in need, and later that morning, as Abram and I entered the grocery store, I handed him a calculator and told him the amount. I explained to him that there were kids his exact age — other thirteen-year-olds living just a few miles away — who didn't have food to eat. I told him that the reason we were taking time out of our Saturday to buy groceries was because following Jesus means you meet needs that he asks you to meet.

"But following Jesus also means we have to be wise with the resources he entrusts to us," I continued. "So I want you to help me figure out how to get the most food for the amount of money we plan to spend, deal?" With that, his little brain went to work. We traipsed up and down nearly every aisle, stuffing our cart with kid-friendly fare, and when it was all said and done, we were only two bucks over budget. "Success!" I said, high-fiving my elated son.

I am trying to teach Abram the lesson I must continue learning myself: you can't give what you don't have, and when a need comes up that God asks you to help meet, you're going to wish you had something to give. Even with his pittance of an allowance, we talk about how Abram can set at least something aside for divine emergencies — a compassion fund of sorts. I tell him that I do the same.

I've been in great need in my life before, and thankfully, people were moved by compassion to help rescue me from my pit. I'm sure it wasn't *convenient* for them. But still, they stopped whatever they were doing, they stepped in with resources they had reserved, and they helped a weaker, wobblier version of me find stable footing once more. The Good Samaritan's example reminds us that we're not called to a life of convenience; we're called to compassion and grace. Who knows what pits that Samaritan had known in his life, but I'd be willing to bet he had known a few. It's always the ones who stay in touch with their own story of being rescued by compassion who render compassion to people they meet. The moment we lose touch with our own broken past is the moment we kiss compassion goodbye.

The Good Samaritan was moved by *compassion*, plain and simple. It's the very thing God hopes will move us too. God's wish for his sons and daughters is that they will rise up and meet the needs they see. They will focus on the single mom, the out-of-work dad, the widow, the orphan, the addict, the one who doesn't quite fit in, asking, "How can I be part of the solution here? What's in my hands to give?" They don't wait for the government to sort out some official program. They jump in — right then — and help.

Not to be a downer here, but we are promised more tough times ahead. There *will* be more tornadoes. There *will* be more tsunamis. There *will* be more widows left to figure out life without their mates. We live in a dangerous, broken world whose needs aren't going away anytime soon.

But I say, if it's true that troubles will *always* be with us — poverty, dejection, heartbreak, not to mention natural disasters galore — then let's *always* have resources available to meet the needs of the people affected by those troubles. Let's live in favor of inconvenience, eager to love and to give and to serve.

44

THE HIGH STAKES
OF SONSHIP

During his illustrious career, Joe Paterno was considered the grandfather of college football—"JoePa," he was called, an entire nation's beloved grandpa. Having worked on the coaching staff for Penn State's Nittany Lions football program since 1949, he is currently the winningest Division I coach ever to live. Sixty-plus years in a leadership role with no scandals to report is impressive in any industry these days, and scandal free is exactly what JoePa was—at least, until this week.

As I write, headlines are being dominated by news of Paterno's longtime right-hand man and famed defensive coordinator, Jerry Sandusky, being charged with sexually abusing at least eight boys, following a grand jury investigation that also led to charges being filed against two university officials who allegedly covered up the abuse. In his first interview after being charged with forty counts of child sex abuse, Sandusky denied any wrongdoing, saying, "I'm not a pedophile ... but I shouldn't have showered with those kids."[21]

Another member of the coaching staff went on record as saying that years ago he had entered the program's locker room to find Sandusky performing a sex act on a ten-year-old boy. The incident had been reported to Paterno, who then accepted the slap on the wrist Sandusky received from higher-ups as sufficient punishment and continued his association with his longtime friend.

Paterno said that he would retire at the football season's conclusion, but the university's board of trustees had a different plan. The court of public opinion had already ruled that Paterno should have done more to protect those victimized kids from harm; as a result, at age eighty-four, the country's favorite grandpa was fired. Shortly thereafter he died.

According to grand jury testimony, Sandusky, now sixty-seven, had abused the children over a fifteen-year period. But these weren't just *any* children. They were at-risk boys attending the philanthropy Sandusky founded, The Second Mile, which is self-described as "a state non-profit organization for children who need additional support and who would benefit from positive human contact."[22]

To exploit vulnerable children is a unique sort of evil, especially exploitation by perpetrators tasked with raising up young boys and girls to reach their potential and their dreams. It's a *stunning* breach of morality, a denial of the very thing mentors are called to do.

✦✧✦

It is estimated that in this country alone, more than fifty-five thousand children are sexually molested each year[23] — innocent, defenseless girls and boys who then grow up wounded, distrusting, and prone to believing the lie that they are worthless and useless and weak. There's an equally tragic outcome for the adults who so viciously harm them: the pain they cause lives on in their own lives and is often passed on to their offspring. The Bible is clear that the consequences of one generation's acts fall for good or for ill on the next generation.

Luke 19 recounts Jesus' heralded arrival at Jerusalem, a city he dearly loved. As he approached the city's gates, he wept. "You've forgotten what alone can bring you peace," he reminded the people. "And now you're vulnerable to attack. The days will come when your enemies will encircle you on every side. They will dash you to the ground, you and the children within your walls. You will never survive their attack, because you've neglected to put God on your side" (Luke 19:41–44, author's abridgment).

The Messiah could say the very same for us.

As a country, we have forgotten what alone will usher in peace in our hearts and in our homes, in our friendships and in our families, in our institutions and in our industries—as well as in our football programs. We have neglected to do the one thing that brings uprightness and integrity to life, insisting we don't need God on our side. Our children are suffering as a result.

✢✢✢

For thousands of years, Orthodox Jews have recited portions of the Old Testament known as the Shema twice daily as a means of affirming their faith. The first passage, from Deuteronomy 6:4–9, reads as follows:

> Hear, O Israel: The LORD our God, the LORD is one. Love the LORD your God with all your heart and with all your soul and with all your strength. These commandments that I give you today are to be on your hearts. Impress them on your children. Talk about them when you sit at home and when you walk along the road, when you lie down and when you get up. Tie them as symbols on your hands and bind them on your foreheads. Write them on the doorframes of your houses and on your gates.

The Shema provides helpful instruction for adults on living life as it's meant to be lived. It also describes the cycle we are supposed to perpetuate for our kids. Love God, it says, with everything you've got. Know God's Word and talk about God's Word and impress holy themes on kids' hearts. Do this in the morning, do this at night, do this when you're driving your children to school and when you're hanging out with them at home. At every moment of every day, let your words, your attitudes, your actions, and your reactions model for the generation coming behind you how to honor God with your life.

I spoke at a leadership retreat for the men of New Life Church several weeks ago, and following the Saturday evening talk on this subject of parenting not only the kids living in our homes but our spiritual children as well, a man approached me.

"I know I've abdicated my role as a spiritual father by some of the choices I've made in my life," he said. "How do I regain that ground? Where do I even start?"

In response, I offered the same twofold answer that Eugene Peterson recites whenever he's asked to define the role of pastor: "Pay attention. And call attention. That's all you need to do."

Sons *pay* attention to what the Father says, to what he is doing in the world. Then they *call* attention to what it looks like to join God in his work.

"Wake up every morning," I advised this negligent dad, "and ask, 'Father, what are you up to today?' It doesn't have to be more complicated than that; God will show you where you can have maximum impact as a parent, a leader, a mentor, a friend — if only you'll *ask* him before you *act*."

The longer I talked, the more agitated this guy became. I could tell from his fidgeting that he was eager for me to get to the part of my answer that included seven quick steps to success. But those steps would never come, because there are no steps. There is no formula. There is no shortcut to listening to God. Sons and daughters *lean in*, remember? They slow their pace, they crane their ear, they commune intentionally with their Dad. And then they busy themselves doing exactly what the Father has asked them to do.

Listen, the stakes of sonship and daughtership have never been higher than they are right now. Millions of kids crave an example that, should they follow it, will show them the path to success. It's up to people like you and me—spiritual dads and spiritual moms—to teach them faithfulness, godliness, responsiveness, obedience, and unflinching self-control. But we'll never be able to pass along habits we have refused to adopt ourselves. The opportunity before us is to love our kids as we ourselves are loved by God—purely, righteously, excellently, with not even a *hint* of malicious intent.

45

FATHERED SONS
FATHER WELL

O ver the past few years, I have been getting to know a young man in our church named Chad. He is twenty-eight years old and single, still lives with his mom, and works part-time as an hourly employee at a nondescript job here in town. By his own choosing, he's disconnected from community, and by his own admission, rather cynical about God. He's a drifter. A nomad. A man without a place to belong.

Chad seems to want to interact, but simultaneously, I can tell, he's suspicious of me. I am a leader, and I am male, and the last male leader he had — his father — bailed on him early in life. But still, he seeks me out. And with every conversation, his eyes search mine with "Please don't hurt me" written in their gaze.

Chad wants to fit in. He wants to find love. He wants to know how to get home — *spiritually* home. Soul-ishly home. He craves the embrace of his Dad.

These days, guys like Chad aren't the exception. Sadly, they are becoming the rule.

In her book *Manning Up*, author Kay Hymowitz writes about the rising prevalence of a stage in a young person's life she dubs "pre-adulthood." Between their lack of responsibilities and an entertainment industry poised to cater to their every pleasure, today's twentysomethings, left to their own devices, have no real motivation to grow up. Citing one simple marker of people's propensity to settle down, the author points out that in 1970, just 16 percent of Americans ages twenty-five to twenty-nine had never been married; today that's true of an astonishing 55 percent of the age group.

"For all its familiarity," she says, "pre-adulthood represents a momentous sociological development. It's no exaggeration to say that having large numbers of single young men and women living independently, while also having enough disposable income to avoid ever messing up their kitchens, is something entirely new in human experience. Yes, at other points in Western history young people have waited well into their twenties to marry, and yes, office girls and bachelor lawyers have been working and finding amusement in cities for more than a century. But their numbers and their money supply were always relatively small. Today's pre-adults are a different matter. They are a major demographic event."[24]

All I would add to Hymowitz's astute assessment is the underlying reason *why*. I'm noticing a trend of my own these days, as I interact with guys such as Chad, which is that men who have been fathered well tend to father well in return. And I'm not just talking about how men raise their biological children. Well-fathered young men carry "father" in a spiritual sense to a largely unfathered world. Let me show you what I mean.

Daniel is another young man at New Life whom I consider to be a friend. Like Chad, he is also twenty-eight. But unlike Chad, he is married, he and his wife are expecting their third child, he owns a house, he has a stable job, and he recently started his own business on the side. Daniel spends his days with intention, working to sort out God's will for his life.

Not surprisingly, Daniel grew up with a dad who was committed to fathering well.

To be clear, outward trappings alone do not define a daughter or a son. Daniel's marriage, his kids, his home, and his job do not automatically declare him a son. It's what stands *behind* those things that proves he is living as a child of God: Confidence. Clarity. Courage. Risk. Daniel knows who he is. He knows *whose* he is. And he's seizing life with passion as a result.

While Chad approaches relationships with skepticism, Daniel jumps in with both feet. When Daniel found the girl he wanted to marry, he mustered the courage to ask for her hand. From there, he committed to responsibly raising children with his wife—no small thing. He took the risk to purchase a house instead of bunking in his parents' basement or renting an apartment for years on end. He then exhibited undeniable confidence in launching a business instead of relegating himself to working for someone else for the rest of his days. His self-concept, informed by God, sets him up for success in every aspect of life.

But back to my point: While Daniel is an excellent father to his children, even more impressive to me is how he carries "father" to people in our church and beyond. Daniel is bold. He is purposeful. He focuses on others. He is resourceful. He comes alongside guys who have never had a role model and shows them what it means to be "son."

Fathered sons father well—there are no truer words than these.

＊✕＊

My dad was a real man's man, but he never shied away from showing affection to his kids. Long after I became an adult, my dad would embrace me and kiss me and shower me with loving words. He would wrap those big strong arms around me and say, "I couldn't be prouder of you, Son."

I read verses such as Isaiah 41:10, in which God talks about upholding his children who are fearful or discouraged or dismayed with his "righteous right hand," and I have no trouble believing that to be true. It's easy for me to consider what it means to be safe in the palm of God's hand, because every day of my life I have felt protected by the hands of my dad. He used his hands to bless me. He used his words to encourage me. He used his actions to provide for me, and his reactions to help me grow into a godly man.

As a result, it's no leap for me to feel fathered by God. But I know not everyone shares my story. Not everyone has had an earthly dad who is kind and gentle and good. Millions of people alive today—men and women alike—are more like Chad than Daniel. They want to fit in. They want to find love. They want to know how to get home. They're out there scrapping and scrounging and raising kids of their own, hoping that somewhere along the way, the gaping hole in their heart gets patched.

✻

A woman who grew up in foster care put it this way: "Parenting without having positive role models is harder than I imagined. Of course, I had other types of models, so to speak: One foster mother was cold and controlling and never touched me if she could help it. Another was overwhelmed and mostly absent. A third really wanted a baby, cooing and gurgling and precious, not a shell-shocked schoolgirl [like me]. When I look back at my childhood, I think of it as war duty, the time I did in the trenches. Not all of me made it out alive."[25]

I'm realizing more and more, as I live this thing called life, that one of the foremost responsibilities I carry as a child of the King is to father people around me who need his care. I can be frustrated, irritated, and inconvenienced by the fact that they don't have it all together. Or I can view my role as a high calling, to be a conduit of God's radical love. Love that accepts. Love that embraces. Love that gets messy. Love that understands. Love that forgives. Love that teaches. Love that rebukes. Love that encourages. Love that says, "Welcome home."

This is the love of our Father. And it's this love that we can provide.

46

ON RESPONDING, RETALIATING, AND SETTING THE RECORD STRAIGHT

S everal years ago, shortly after I accepted the New Life post, things were said about me in the media that were patently false. This didn't happen just once; it happened several times, and one day I had had enough. With that morning's errant newspaper online edition still staring back at me from my laptop's screen, I plotted my revenge. I would find this careless reporter and demand that he print a new story to set the record straight. I would clear up his "facts," fix his flawed findings, and hopefully save a little face.

But thankfully, better judgment prevailed. After taking a few deep breaths and asking God for a little wisdom, I picked up the phone to call my mentor-friend Jimmy Evans, who pastors in Amarillo. That's usually how I address any crisis that befalls my life: breathe, pray, call Jimmy — in that order.

I explained the situation to my longtime friend, including what I was thinking about saying to the reporter in my defense. "I just need to get this off my chest," I told him, "and then let the chips fall where they may."

Jimmy said nothing, so I kept ranting. "I'm tired of being criticized for something I didn't do, you know? The more I mull it over, the more I think I *have* to respond."

Again, nothing, which is one of the things I love about Jimmy. I can call him and vent with all the strength and passion I feel, without fearing any reprisal whatsoever. This is a man who listens well.

But he also knows when to speak.

"Brady," he said after a dramatic pause, "there is a difference between being defensive and being a defender."

I could tell by his measured tone, his carefully chosen words, that the conversation was quickly headed in a direction I didn't necessarily want it to go. Where was the fun in rational thinking, when *revenge* was ours to be had?

"Hmmm," I said, his comment still hanging uncomfortably in the air. "All right, I'll bite. Tell me what you mean."

He spoke even slower than his usual drawl allowed for. "Brady, only you know what's behind your frustration. Answer me this: Does your anger center on protecting your reputation, or does it center on protecting the people you have been called to pastor?"

I sat back in my chair. Exhaled my annoyance. Rubbed the bridge of my nose. "The church is fine," I finally admitted. Then, after a beat, "This is about me."

Jimmy advised me that I'd be wise to not utter a word. "If the church is being slandered, step forward and defend your flock," he said. "That's what shepherds do — they protect their sheep from wolves. But if this is just about your reputation, relax. Let God defend you instead."

Something deep inside me wanted to scream, *But what they're reporting — it's all a bunch of lies!*

✦✢✦

It's easy to be a defender when life is coming up roses. Have you noticed that? When your day is stuffed with attaboys, you have no need to flex the revenge muscle. But take that same twenty-four-hour period and insert one teensy word of criticism, and watch how quickly the defender turns defensive.

Defensive about your motives.

Defensive about your reputation.

Defensive about your attitudes, your actions, your name.

Or is it just me that this happens to?

Daughters and sons are defenders who leave defensiveness to somebody else. They recognize that the moment they surrendered themselves to the lordship of Jesus Christ, their reputation and livelihood literally died. They are dead men walking. Dead women walking. All they have now is Christ's. All they have now is *Christ*.

But what a marvelous thing to have.

During my little chat with Jimmy, I was reminded that I'm not working to build a Brady Boyd brand. I'm working to glorify *God*. I have no reputation except his. I am his and he is mine—isn't that what the cross is all about? He purchased me so that the Father and I could be one, just as the Son and the Father are one. Brady in his former self has left the building; now all that remains—thankfully—is Christ.

After Jimmy and I ended our call, and after my ranting had mercifully died down, I thought through the wisdom in the words of 1 Peter 2. I had devoured the passage before but never savored it as much as I did now. "When they hurled their insults at him," the apostle Peter wrote, referring to Jesus, "he did not retaliate; when he suffered, he made no threats. Instead, he entrusted himself to him who judges justly. 'He himself bore our sins' in his body on the cross, so that we might die to sins and live for righteousness; 'by his wounds you have been healed.' For 'you were like sheep going astray,' but now you have returned to the Shepherd and Overseer of your souls" (vv. 23–25).

As I scanned those words for the umpteenth time, I sensed God saying to me, *You want to know what the underlying root of your insecurity is? The reason why you're so fired up about what these reporters are writing about you? Somewhere along the way, you convinced yourself that you'd never get insulted in life. But to associate with my Son is to invite massive criticism—most of which is hardly deserved.*

Jimmy's parting comments carried this same idea. "When you took the job at New Life," he said, "you painted a giant bull's-eye on your chest. If you're not going to be a big boy about the criticism you receive, then let the church hire somebody else. Insults are going to continue to be hurled at you. Your job is to figure out how you'll respond."

Everybody needs a friend like Jimmy Evans. We all need to be reined in sometimes.

✛⚮✛

I stared at the words of 1 Peter 2 in the open Bible on my desk for several minutes longer and was drawn to verse 25: "For 'you were like sheep going astray,' but now you have returned to the Shepherd and Overseer of your souls."

Did I really trust God to oversee my soul? Or was I determined to do his job for him by responding, retaliating, insisting on setting the record straight? The truth was tough to take.

✛⚮✛

I'm learning a couple of things these days about how to let God be God in my life. First, I now realize that I'm most vulnerable to feelings of insecurity when I'm walking through a season of significant change. Criticism—especially when it comes from a reporter's pen—is never fun. But it carries a special sting when I'm operating off my normal routine. During a typical week, I have systems in place for staying connected to Christ, my family, my friends, my staff, and my goals regarding finances, health, and growth. But toss a new role, a new city, a new house in the mix, and those systems take a hit. As a result, I'm thrown off balance. I'm uncertain. I'm self-doubting. I'm tired. This is when Satan *loves* to strike. Simply knowing when to watch out for my enemy helps me block his predictable blow.

Second, I'm learning that there is safety in numbers where vengeance is concerned. Specifically, the more I can hang around secure, measured, kind people, the more those tendencies rub off on me. Secure people live free from anxiety and fear. They are immovable, unshakeable, firm. And they teach me to live this way too.

I am married to the most secure person I know. Pam and I have gone through some of the biggest traumas and crises a couple can face, and yet she remains fixed and steady and sound. When I arrive home each afternoon, I know I'll be walking into an environment marked by peace. There is no drama in the Boyd home, because my bride has done her due diligence on the insecurity front. She has fought the battles she needed to fight in order to prevail secure and strong. As you would imagine, it's a huge gift to be married to someone like that.

Likewise, the senior-most leaders at New Life — the men and women I minister with day in and day out — carry these very same traits. They model for me how to move through adversity with my godliness intact.

✻⚇✻

A third thing I'm learning about becoming a defender is that it's really difficult to stay mad at someone you've decided to pray for instead. I should clarify here that by "pray for," I don't mean "ask God to strike them with oozing boils"; however, even those prayers can be more transformative to the one praying than praying no prayers at all.

There is a country song out right now that starts out as a repentant ballad. A heartbroken guy finds himself sitting in church one Sunday, devastated over his girlfriend walking out on him. For the first time in his life, he's open to advice from a preacher on what to do. "You can't go on hating others who have done wrong to you," the preacher says that day at church. "Sometimes we get angry, but we must not condemn. Let the good Lord do his job, and you just pray for them."

So the guy decides to take the high road and pray for the gal who broke his heart — that her brakes would go out, that a flowerpot would fall from a windowsill and knock her in the head, that her birthday would come and nobody would call, and that her dreams would never come true.

Not exactly the kind of prayers I mean.

Regarding that reporter who nearly sent me over retaliation's edge, my wrath toward him somehow waned once I committed the matter to prayer. I asked God for an opportunity to get to know him. I prayed blessing over his work life, his family, his soul. I confessed my feelings of ill will toward him and asked for compassion to reign instead. I invited God's Spirit to invade my heart and lead me to gratitude and graciousness and peace.

Who knows what God will do in that relationship in coming days? Surely something more beneficial than what would have transpired if I had lambasted the guy instead.

＊✄＊

And then, a fourth lesson, even if more trivial than the first three: A good night's sleep works wonders when you're chomping at the vengeance bit. Before you reply on Facebook or Twitter or email, or are tempted to pick up the phone and attack, go to sleep.

I mean it.

Get a good night's rest and reevaluate things in the light of a brand-new day. Have some quiet time. Join hands with your spouse or your kid or your dog and sing "Kumbaya" if you must. Do anything to recenter yourself so that God has the chance to speak to you. Notice how your anger has diminished. Notice how your perspective has shifted. Notice how your passion for writing a nasty note has been replaced by the urge to repair the relationship instead.

That passage in 1 Peter that I referenced earlier says this: "It is commendable if someone bears up under the pain of unjust suffering because they are conscious of God. But how is it to your credit if you receive a beating for doing wrong and endure it? But if you suffer for doing good and you endure it, this is commendable before God. To this you were called, because Christ suffered for you, leaving you an example, that you should follow in his steps" (2:19–21).

There will be times in our lives when bad things happen that, plainly, just are not just. Sure, if you or I steal money from our employer, then we deserve it when we get fired. Bearing that type of "bad thing" is not commendable before God, because we had it coming. But there will be *other* occasions, Jesus promises, when the fault is not at all ours. And in light of that reality, what we must remember is that we're Christ's possessions now. We're his daughters. We're his sons. We're citizens of a holy nation, members of a royal priesthood, a chosen people belonging to God. What happened to us may not be our burden, but responding appropriately is.

I have noticed that while this is very good theology, it's not frequently taught. Probably because no pastor wants to stand in front of a group of people and say, "Hey, listen, you know this whole Christianity thing? The love-joy-peace-eternity-with-God-in-heaven deal? Well, just to shoot straight, signing up with Jesus also means saying yes to undeserved pain. And God is often far more interested in talking about how you're responding to it than about the unfair hand you're being dealt."

Scores of believers seeking answers have approached me with various forms of the very same question: "Where was God when _____ happened to me?" It may be a job layoff, a spouse walking out, verbal or sexual abuse—and what they want to know, as they look back on the injustice, is why God abandoned them in their greatest time of need.

Where was he? they wonder.

Why didn't he intervene?

Didn't he see I was being mistreated?
Didn't he care?

It can take many years and loads of therapy before some of those folks can believe me when I say, "He was right there." But in fact he was. And he is. And he always will be. In the face of the wonderful and the woeful, God remains right by our side, watching, assessing, embracing, comforting, encouraging, reminding, assuring. *I allowed this situation in order to awaken your heart to me,* he says. *And I never for a moment stopped being the loving Overseer of your soul.*

47

THE PURPOSE
OF FORGIVENESS

I had to endure many bullies during my growing-up years, but the first one — and perhaps the most influential — was a guy named Tony. He was one grade ahead of me and pinpointed me as the sole target of his daily taunts; eventually he encouraged all his friends to follow suit. I was in middle school at the time, and I remember experiencing an emotional whirlwind of fear, disillusionment, humiliation, and rage over the things those boys did to me. They would punch me and kick me, they'd spit at me and taunt me, and one time they dragged me by a rope tied around my neck. I could never sort out in my immature mind what I had done to deserve treatment like that. I just knew that I was being wronged, and I wanted it to stop.

I didn't know much of spiritual things when I was a young teenage boy. In fact, if you had come to me back in my middle school days and said, "Brady, I know the stunts that Tony has pulled have been really hurtful to you, but still, you ought to forgive him," I would have thought you had lost your marbles. Bullies deserved nothing but scorn — of that much, I was sure.

✦⊃✦

The purpose of forgiveness is the same as Jesus' purpose for everything: restoration. He forgave us so that we can be restored to the original plan for our lives. We forgive others so that they can be restored to fellowship, unity, trust. The reason, then, why we *don't* forgive is that we don't really care if they are restored. This apathy resides at the core of every bout of bitterness the human heart has known.

They screwed up.
They wronged me.
They are thoughtless and worthless and cruel.
They deserve whatever's coming to them.
Good riddance, good luck. Goodbye.

We determine that some people are simply beyond the boundaries of forgiveness, and with that we write them off. That's how I felt toward Tony way back when. It's how I'm tempted to feel still today.

But this isn't the way of Christ.

✢✄✢

More than two thousand years ago, and on the heels of three years of fruitful public ministry, our Lord Jesus Christ found himself hanging on a splintered cross. Crucifixion was a vicious form of torture, perfected by the Romans who supervised his death. The way a person died on the cross was not by starvation or penetration wounds or exhaustion. The way you died was by suffocation. Your muscles would give out, your shoulders would dislocate, and you would no longer be able to lift yourself up to catch your breath.

It stands to reason, then, that one of the most difficult things for Jesus to do while he was nailed to the cross was to talk. And yet before he died, he would hoist himself up and through much travail choose to speak. What was so important that Jesus would endure so much pain to get it said? What words could possibly warrant such suffering?

"Father, forgive them," our Savior said, "for they do not know what they are doing" (Luke 23:34).

Father, *forgive them* — this was the heartbeat of Jesus' life and ministry. Forgive the one holding the whip that is ripping flesh clear off my bones. Forgive the one who pierced my head with the crown of thorns. Forgive the ones who are casting lots for my clothing, even as I hang here and die. Forgive people mocking me and ridiculing me and shouting, "Die, king of the Jews!"

Jesus knew that even the most unlikely people could, by his Father's power, be redeemed.

✦╳✦

Luke 17 tells the story of how Jesus, traveling with a crowd of people along the border between Samaria and Galilee, heading to Jerusalem, was met by ten men suffering from leprosy. Verse 12 says the men "stood at a distance" as Jesus was passing by. They had heard that this great healer would be coming through town and allowed themselves a glimmer of hope. *Maybe he can restore us to the life we used to know!*

Leprosy isn't a common ailment today, thanks to advances in medical technology. But in Jesus' time, it destroyed many lives by literally eating away a person's skin. Lepers would often have open sores all over their body and were considered unclean by religious leaders of the day. They were banished from society and had to live in leper colonies on the outskirts of town. They were ostracized from family, from the synagogue, from the community, from life. If they thought they'd been written off by the world, it's because in fact they had been.

Back on the street, the ten lepers called out, "Jesus, Master, have pity on us!" (Luke 17:13). And in a scandalous move, Jesus walked toward — not away from — those ten men. He told them to make their way to the priest, and that in doing so, they would be cleansed. It's as if he said, "You're going to have to blow past the boundaries you've previously known, for restoration to be yours." It takes active faith to offer restoration to someone, and often it takes active faith to be restored.

I can picture those guys walking along the road to the temple. In those days, lepers could be arrested, beaten, and tossed in jail for coming too close to town, and now here they are approaching the *temple*? Was Jesus out of his *mind*?

But still, they go. What else are they going to do? This is their only recourse, according to the world's greatest healer. And so, with trepidation to spare, they courageously take step after step toward new life.

I imagine those lepers studying their skin with each step, just *knowing* that at some point they're going to be cleansed. A few minutes into the walk, Bob looks at Joe and says, "Hey … my hand! Look! It's better than before!" A few steps later Joe elbows Tom and says, "Something feels different. My face … how does my face look?" To which Tom casts a sidelong glance and says, "You know what? You're right! I mean, you're still ugly. But your face— it's actually *healed*."

As they go, they are cleansed. They are restored. They are healed.

This is the ending that Jesus makes available to every story that's ever been lived. We can know perfect cleansing and restoration. We can be made healthy and whole. And so can the modern-day lepers we disregard and cast aside.

✦☙✦

To me, the most fascinating part of this story comes at the very end. The men have been healed, the leprosy is gone, and Jesus goes on his merry way. But he doesn't get far before one of the men rushes up to him, praising him and throwing himself at Jesus' feet. The text makes a point of explaining that this man was a Samaritan, someone who carried as much social stigma back then as undocumented citizens and radical Muslims do today. Of all ten people Jesus chose to heal, the Samaritan was the only one to say thanks. The guy *nobody* would have expected to surrender to Christ proved he wasn't beyond restoration's bounds.

Jesus knew we needed this object lesson, this reminder that it's never wise to eye our enemies and say with confidence, "They'll never change." Sometimes they *do* change. All of them *can* change. Either the gospel can restore everybody, or it cannot restore anybody. Nobody is beyond the reach of forgiveness, restoration, and grace. And I, a world-class sinner, am glad.

✱☓✱

Lately I have been learning that the more grateful I am, the more quickly I tend to forgive. The more I stay in touch with how awful it felt to live apart from God, the more determined I am to see people restored. I want to remember how lonely and purposeless I was before I fully surrendered myself to Christ. I want to return to him day after day and say, "Thank you, Lord, for grace." His intervention in my life when I least deserved it proves that his arm really isn't too short.

"Praise the LORD, my soul; all my inmost being, praise his holy name," Psalm 103 declares. "Praise the LORD, my soul, and forget not all his benefits—who forgives all your sins and heals all your diseases, who redeems your life from the pit and crowns you with love and compassion, who satisfies your desires with good things so that your youth is renewed like the eagle's" (vv. 1–5). What a goal for us as Jesus' followers, to carry this type of message to a world in need: "Your sins can be forgiven! Your diseases can all be healed. Your pitiful life can be redeemed, and your every God-honoring desire can be met." We forgive others because Jesus first forgave us. Not only does our forgiveness help restore the wrongdoer back into fellowship, but as we follow Jesus' model for extending forgiveness, something in us is restored too.

I lost track of Tony, the boy who bullied me, after high school, but the damage he did to me stuck around for quite some time in my heart. It wasn't until many years later—after I had married Pam and started a family—that I received the terrible news. Tony, who by that time also had a wife and kids, had tragically taken his own life. As word of his death washed over me, I realized I had never forgiven those wrongs. "Father, I release the bitterness I've been carrying and forgive him in your powerful name," I prayed.

True, there is never a bad time to extend forgiveness. But how I wish I would have done so back when Tony was still alive.

48

THE JONAH SYNDROME

The woman sitting across from me had requested this meeting urgently. "Unusual circumstances," she had said, and indeed they were.

She told her story hurriedly, anxious to pose the pressing question she had brought with her. Unbelievably, her beloved son — a young professional who was an up-and-comer in his field — had been murdered, she explained — robbed, attacked, and drowned in the ocean. To make matters worse, the two killers were still at large. "The men who did this have not been brought to justice, and they definitely committed this crime," she said. Then, after a beat, "I guess I came to ask you what I'm to do in this situation."

She trained her eyes on mine. She had come to a pastor for input on God, and God is a God of justice, right? Surely she was supposed to right this wrong in defense of her innocent son.

I studied her determined face, then leaned forward in my chair. Slowly, cautiously, I said, "I know your motivations are pure, in that you want to see justice prevail. But my advice to you is that above *all* else, you carefully guard your heart."

After letting that comment fill the space between us, I reminded the grieving mom that at some point God would in fact bring everything to justice, and that it was not always our responsibility to help him get that done. "You must believe that he will fulfill justice," I said, "in his own timing and in his own way. The bigger and more immediate challenge you face is ensuring that bitterness and rage are not allowed to take root in your heart."

I can't imagine the pain of losing a child in such a vicious and violent way. I can't *begin* to comprehend the agony of then watching the killers walk away. But no matter what injustices we face in this world, our hearts remain ours, and it remains up to us to decide how we will respond. And this mother was wrestling with what I call the Jonah Syndrome: craving justice most for others while what we crave most for ourselves is grace.

❋

Jonah was a prophet in Israel thousands of years ago, but his story remains well-known today. He was minding his own business, living his everyday life, when God approached him with a mission. Jonah was to travel by boat to a secular town called Nineveh and deliver a message on God's behalf. "Repent, or judgment is coming," he was to tell them. "In forty days your city will be overthrown." And tell them he did. He took a detour through the belly of a very large fish, but eventually he got the job done.

The people of Nineveh were wicked folks, and Jonah agreed with God that they should be wiped from the face of the earth. But to Jonah's immense disappointment, God relented and spared them instead.

"Repent, or judgment is coming!" Jonah had cried. To his surprise, they *did* repent.

Jonah climbed to the top of a nearby hill and looked down on the city whose once-deviant leaders were now desperately seeking God. Wearing sackcloth and ashes, they begged God to change their hearts. All the while, Jonah looked on in disbelief. Where was the *justice* they so deserved?

He looked heavenward and said to God, "I knew it! I *knew* you were going to have mercy on this people and not do what you said you would do. I did my part. I came all the way here and told them what you said to say. *You*, on the other hand, promised judgment and justice, and now you're just sitting there, letting them repent! These people deserve your strongest *wrath*, not the gift of a brand-new start."

We crave justice most for others while what we crave most for ourselves is grace.

✦❍✦

I can't read the account of Jonah without thinking about my sister. We are very close in age, and growing up, I remember feeling elated whenever she got punished. I would push my ear to the door and relish each swat as it made contact with her rear end. *Pow!* She'd whimper and wait for the next, while I was in the hall giggling. Nice brother, huh?

I'm sure you would be tempted to judge me, except that you probably did the same thing too. And why were we so happy? Because *justice* was being served. We love it when people who screw up get their due, unless the screwup happens to be us.

Even if we nod in agreement at the idea that someday ultimate justice will be served and that God—not we—should serve it, something in us stays skeptical. We want justice served *right now*. We want to champion it, fight for it, see it served today. We want to exhale with the satisfaction of knowing we somehow brought it to pass. And therein lies the problem. We take a central, divine characteristic that belongs solely to our heavenly Father, and we twist the situation to make it all about us.

I think there's a better way.

✦✄✦

The more wounds I pick up in this raggedy life, the more I see that if I beg for justice for the ones who wrong me, I tend to receive justice myself. But if I beg for grace for them, I get much-needed grace too. And the older I get, the more I realize that I really *like* things like grace. I want the help that God offers. I want the rescue afforded to me by his Son. I enjoy seeing justice served to the deserving, but as for me, I would like to live life under grace.

And so I come to God, again and again, asking grace for people who are least worthy of it, asking for justice to stay its hand. I ask God to heal my craving for justice and to expand my desire for grace. I remind him of the ones who have hurt me, and clarify for him that *still* he has not made it right. And then I beg him with all sincerity to give me the strength to let it go. I take a deep breath. I let my shoulders fall. I rise from that time of prayer and walk away, leaving my justice-bent behind.

"Give me faith today to believe you, Lord, when you say you will set all things right. And in the meantime, heal me fully. Let me live as a carrier of grace."

49

BISCUITS AND GRAVY, WITH A SIDE OF SILENCE

As I have mentioned, my kids and I have a weekend ritual every Saturday morning, when I take either Abram or Callie out for breakfast. The following week, it's the other one's turn. On Abram's days, we head to a greasy spoon a few miles north of our house, where he orders the Number 7 — eggs, bacon, and a huge cinnamon roll, with a large hot chocolate to drink. My son will probably never alter his order, because his favorite part of the experience is scooting up his stool to the café's bar and saying to our waitress, "The usual, please." We have the same server every time, and she always responds to Abram with a grin and a southern-drawled, "You got it, Sugar."

When Abram knows it's his turn for breakfast with Dad, he is up early, gets dressed lightning fast, and climbs into my truck at seven sharp. We get to the restaurant, we head for our typical spot, and I listen while he talks and talks and talks. He has a million thoughts flowing through his young mind, and he can't wait to convey them (all of them) to Dad. We talk and we laugh and we brainstorm ideas, and by the time we arrive back home, we are spent.

If Abram is eager, effusive, and excited to speak his mind, Callie is just the opposite.

On Callie's Saturdays, it takes half a dozen reminders that it's time to go. She's not unenthusiastic about our dates; she just doesn't share her brother's deep appreciation for punctuality, precision, and early-morning appointments. Eventually my daughter and I load into the truck and head to Cracker Barrel, where she orders her standard biscuits and gravy, and we proceed to exchange *maybe* a dozen sentences.

After an hour or so, we head back home, where Pam asks Callie how it went. With eyes beaming and smile wide, Callie always says, "Great!" and means it, while I stand nearby thinking, *It was? We barely even talked!*

Earlier this summer, the air was unseasonably cool one evening, and I asked Callie if she wanted to go outside and build a fire in our little backyard fire pit. She was thrilled, and so we bundled up and headed out. She has her own hatchet—a small, dull one that couldn't do damage to a stick of soft butter—and we were out there gathering kindling and then bigger pieces of wood, which she would hack at and toss in the fire.

We must have been out there for an hour—Callie contentedly chopping up firewood and building her flame toward the sky, while I watched from a chair by the fire—and neither of us said a word. It's not wordy paragraphs that reach my daughter; it's simply the presence of her dad.

✂

I'm learning something as I walk through these years with my kids. They are individuals carefully crafted by the hand of a loving God, not cookie-cutter children stamped out by a mold. So I can choose to see and value their uniqueness, or I can single-handedly squelch their souls.

Proverbs 22:6 is an oft-quoted verse that says, "Train up a child in the way he should go: and when he is old, he will not depart from it" (KJV). Most parents take that exhortation to mean we should stuff as much knowledge about God into our little ones' lives as early and as often as possible, so that they will grow up to be responsible adults who do not cuss and do not steal.

There is some truth to that: kids who grow up learning about morals and values and ethics and what it means to follow Jesus instead of going their own way in life *do* stand a better chance of keeping a low tally of sins. But there is a deeper meaning to that verse. Here is how the Amplified Bible conveys the bigger idea: "Train up a child in the way he should go [and in keeping with his individual gift or bent], and when he is old he will not depart from it."

Our role as moms and dads has far more to do with tapping into our kids' uniqueness than with simply teaching them right versus wrong. Abram and Callie and every other child on the planet each has a bent formed by the hand of God. It's our job as parents to draw it out. I can't parent my daughter the same way I parent my son; they require *custom care* from their dad. And as I get better at adapting my approach, I see my kids coming alive. Our heavenly Father regards us each uniquely; my goal is to offer my children the very same gift.

50

TO SMELL OF
BOURBON AND SMOKE

Shortly after I became New Life's senior pastor, I agreed to do a phone interview with a radio station regarding my plans for leading the church. As soon as the program's host wrapped up our dialogue, he asked if I'd be willing to take a few questions from callers. I second-guessed my cheery reply when I heard the first caller's opening remark. In a flat, defiant tone she said, "I've never met a Christian I liked."

Before I could respond, she then asked rather sarcastically, "Would I even be *welcomed* at New Life Church?"

Taken aback, I said, "Wow. Tell me why you ask."

"Because I'm a pagan Druid," she said.

At the time, I had no idea what a pagan Druid was, so I requested some clarification. I would learn that modern Druidry is a nature-based religion of sorts that believes in reincarnation, among other things. In all honesty, her explanation didn't matter. She would have been welcomed at New Life Church regardless of her response. I told her as much, and then I said, "In fact, why don't you come this weekend and sit with my wife and me? Come hang out with us. We'll save you a spot. We sit on the front row every week, and we would be honored to host you."

There was a pregnant pause. Then, with genuine surprise, she said, "Really?"

"Absolutely," I said. "Pam and I would love for you to worship with us. You are more than welcome to join us on Sunday."

Her voice shifted from cynical to sweet. "Well ... okay. Thank you. Truly. Thanks for the invitation."

We ended our conversation, and for a few seconds I felt pretty good about how things were panning out. But then came call number two.

The amped-up man's exact words were, "You're just gonna love her right into *hell*, aren't ya!"

After a brief pause, he went on. "I'll tell you what you need to do! You need to tell that last caller that she's a *sinner*, that she's going to *hell*, and that she needs *Jesus*!"

I inhaled to proffer a response, but before I could get it out, he reiterated his point: "You're just another pastor who is fine with *loving* people right into *hell*!"

Finally sensing an opening, I took a deep breath and said, "You know, I think I now know why that first caller was so upset. I wonder if you are one of the Christians she met along the way. Sir, it was love, not threats of impending judgment, that originally drew me to Christ. I will not love that woman into hell. Hopefully, as a church, we will love her into heaven."

The caller evidently didn't have anything to say, so I continued. "Interestingly, the only people Jesus ever really got mad at were people uncannily similar to you—angry church people. I don't want to live that way—do you?"

The tone was civil as we exchanged a few closing remarks, and I was all but ready to be done with the whole deal, when call number three rang in. It was the Druid again. "Hey," she said, "I'm so sorry about all of this. I heard your last caller, and I certainly didn't mean to stir up a hornet's nest. Anyway, I wanted to call and thank you again for saying what you said, and for being the first Christian I might just like."

✦⚇✦

Luke 7 tells the story of a dinner party. Evidently, a group of Pharisees and Jesus were reclining at the dinner table when a well-known sinful woman entered the home unannounced. It was common in those days for passersby to invite themselves in when the door was ajar, so it wasn't her mere presence that incited Jesus' hosts. It was what happened after she was inside that proved scandalous.

Verse 38 says that "as she stood behind him [Jesus] at his feet weeping, she began to wet his feet with her tears. Then she wiped them with her hair, kissed them and poured perfume on them."

When the Pharisee who had invited Jesus over saw this, he was shocked. Didn't Jesus know that the woman touching him was a vile sinner? What was he thinking, letting her weep on him and then use her own hair as a towel to mop up her filthy mess?

Jesus looked at the men seated before him — unwittingly, they were behaving as spiritual slaves — and cleared up their confusion. *They* hadn't given him water for his feet, he explained, but the sinful woman had. *They* hadn't given him a kiss, but the sinful woman had. *They* hadn't anointed him with oil, but the sinful woman had. "I tell you," he said, "her many sins have been forgiven — as her great love has shown. But whoever has been forgiven little loves little." He then looked into the woman's eyes and said, "Your sins are forgiven.... Your faith has saved you; go in peace" (vv. 47–50).

Jesus knew that surrender had led her to the place of "daughter." It's where she had needed to be all along. What's more, he knew the kind of advocate she would now be for this far-better way of life. People who have been forgiven much know how to forgive much. Those who have been loved well know how to love well.

Those who have been welcomed in, despite their many failings and flaws, know how to extend a hand of friendship to the outcast, the downcast, the rejected, and the banned.

❧

The first Sunday of 2011, we had Vision Sunday at New Life. It was a time for us to reaffirm our vision and values by telling stories of God's faithfulness the previous year. One story in particular highlighted our Father's constant care.

In 2010, a couple in our church was going through a rough time financially. The husband-and-wife team, Clark and Carol, owned a high-end custom cabinet business that they had built from the ground up, but their once-thriving enterprise was tanking in a down economy. It had been more than a year since they had received a paycheck, and things weren't looking promising for income anytime soon.

In the midst of that season of struggle, one Saturday afternoon when Clark was leaving his downtown office, he saw a man walking aimlessly down the street who appeared to be down on his luck. Clark was prompted to strike up a conversation with the man, which is how he learned that the man had recently lost his wife and in desperation had decided to try to drink himself to death. He didn't have the courage to shoot himself, he said, but he had spent the last several months getting bourbon any way he could and then downing as much of the bottle as his stomach could hold, before passing out cold where he lived.

The man then revealed to Clark that his wife's final words haunted him every single day. "On her deathbed," he said, "she told me that one day I would join her in heaven. She said there was no way I would be able to outrun God."

Sonship, his wife was promising him, a promise his orphan ears couldn't receive. The man looked at Clark and said, "Guess you could say I'm hell-bent on proving her wrong."

Clark took in the man's story, his momentary sobriety, his pleading eyes, and then smiled, saying, "Let me see what I can do."

Clark and Carol were hurdling their own challenging financial obstacles, but they were compelled to do something to help. They located temporary housing for their newfound friend—Larry, he'd said his name was—landed him a paying job, and scrounged together four hundred dollars toward the purchase of a car. Then they called me.

After explaining the situation, Clark said, "Pastor Brady, Carol and I found a car for six hundred bucks. If we chip in four hundred, can New Life fund the rest?" After verifying that such an inexpensive car did in fact come with a working engine and useful features such as wheels and seats, I told him we would be happy to help. In two minutes flat, the deal was done.

Despite their own messiness, Clark and Carol climbed into another person's mess. Classic son-and-daughter behavior.

Later I asked Clark how things were going. Not only had Larry stepped off the path leading to a slow suicide, but also he had surrendered his life to Jesus Christ during the Christmas season at New Life. He was holding down his job and was no longer living month to month. I asked Clark if he and Larry would be willing to share their story with the congregation as a way to encourage our church.

Sunday morning—Vision Sunday—was to be the big day. Just before the first service, Clark approached me and said, "Uh, Brady, we might have a problem." He explained that although Larry really had been trying his best to follow Jesus, evidently he was so nervous about speaking on a stage in front of thousands of people that he drank all night long before heading up to the church. "He reeks of alcohol and is barely sober," Clark said, a flash of panic in his eyes.

I said, "Well, is he going to do anything inappropriate up on stage?" to which Clark replied, "Absolutely not. The guy is *terri-*

fied. He's willing to relay his story, but I'm telling you, he really smells like booze and smoke."

As it turned out, Clark was right. I stood onstage between the two men, drawing the story out of them, and each time I turned toward Larry, the odor of bourbon and stale tobacco smoke filled my nose. But here's what I thought throughout that entire interview: I love this church. I love this collection of very messy people who make room for still other people's messes. I hope this place *always* reeks of bourbon, if it means a single soul is pointed toward Christ.

Sometimes the path to full surrender is marked not by giant leaps but by baby steps. It may have been true for you. It certainly was true for me. Sons and daughters have been welcomed by a gracious, loving God who held his arms open wide, even as they baby-stepped their way toward him. And now those same children of the King enjoy nothing more than to be welcoming to people who are searching for the path leading them home.

51

FOREVER AND ALWAYS
FAMILY

Three years ago my assistant, Karla, and her husband, Brandon, adopted a little girl named Alisa from Colorado's foster care system. After all the paperwork had been completed, Pam and I headed down to the El Paso County courthouse, where a judge would legalize the pact before Karla and Brandon's family and friends.

Near the end of the proceedings, the judge did something I thought was brilliant. She called five-year-old Alisa up to her side — right there on the bench — and put her gavel in front of the young child. She then asked Alisa, "Do you want Karla and Brandon to be your parents — your forever and always family?"

Alisa eyed the judge, who was smiling, and then cracked a smile of her own. She gathered up the judge's gavel with both hands and held it over its large wooden base. "Alisa," the judge confirmed, "as soon as you bang down that gavel, I am going to decree that you are a permanent member of Karla and Brandon's family." Still grinning from ear to ear, Alisa brought down the gavel with a five-year-old's full force; and with one strike of the block, abandoned orphan became cherished child. Alisa was finally home — officially, permanently, joyously. Her deepest needs, at last, could be met.

To be accepted and adored, to be nurtured and known, to be listened to and led in God's perfect will—deep inside *every* soul, these cravings all strain to be fed.

❧

Watching Alisa become a legal member of Karla and Brandon's family carried real significance for me. Several years prior, Pam and I had been the ones standing before a judge during the adoption of our son. "Who here wants to raise this boy as their own?" that judge had asked, to which my bride and I exclaimed in unison, "We do!"

"Congratulations, and good luck," he said. And with that, Abram was ours. Another gavel had come down. Another adoption had been declared final. Another orphan was welcomed home.

The whole transaction was a blur until several weeks later, when we received Abram's birth certificate in the mail. I stared at that form for many minutes, specifically at the contents of the little box titled "Name": *Abram Neal Boyd*, it read. Abram is a *Boyd*, I thought. Officially. Permanently. Joyously.

The excitement and pride that puffed up my chest that day must be akin to what God feels whenever one of his kids chooses at last to come home. Everyone born into this life is born with a gavel in his or her hands. One day, we either pound it down in favor of joining God's family, or we leave it suspended in midair—and in doing so, say no to God.

In August of 1988, I banged that gavel confidently and surrendered my life to Christ. Admittedly, it felt risky: Could I trust God with my future? Was his way really better than mine? But his Spirit had piqued my interest. How was I supposed to say no when I was compelled toward an earnest *yes*?

I made the right decision that day, and I have never once looked back.

This is how salvation goes, isn't it? We get to say our "Yes!" with gusto, swinging the gavel down with conviction, instead of staying the skeptic, orphaned by doubt. We get to opt into God's forever family, rather than frittering our days away searching for home. Regarding people who come under Christ's authority, the apostle Paul said, "You're no longer wandering exiles. This kingdom of faith is now your home country. You're no longer strangers or outsiders. You *belong* here" (Eph. 2:19 MSG, emphasis added).

It's not just that we get heaven when this life gives way to the next. We also gain the care of a family—right here, right now, today. We become part of a family that includes us and inspires us, encourages us and emboldens us, trains us up in righteousness and reminds us who we are.

When I was a kid, there were certain house rules that we observed because we were Boyds. Boyds did certain things and Boyds *didn't* do others—my parents were clear about that. We didn't wrestle in the house, for example. We didn't talk back to Mom and Dad. And whenever we spoke to somebody older than ourselves, it was a given that we would say "Sir" or "Ma'am." We were grateful for every resource we had and were helpful to people in need. We used words as gifts, not weapons, and we did what we said we would do. This, in part, is what it meant to be a Boyd. It is just who we were.

Similarly, when we join God's household of faith, we get exposed to the inner workings of the home. Scripture brims with explanations of how our heavenly Father intends for us to live: choosing him over all other gods, honoring life in all its forms, expressing thanks for what we find in our own hands instead of taking what belongs to someone else, working hard and resting consistently, treating people with dignity and kindness, carrying hope with us wherever we go in this world, remembering whose cause we're fighting for, and serving God with all of our strength. The list goes on, but hopefully the point is clear: each time you and I choose acceptance over ostracism, love over hate, faith over fear, kindness over spite, we reaffirm that initial strike of the gavel, when we declared that we are his.

52

HERE LIES
A GRATEFUL SHEEP

Throughout the Bible, heaven is spoken of as a pretty cool place to be. For starters, only the redeemed will be there, which means it will be a place of unity and harmony and grace. What's more, because there will be not a single ounce of sin present—no struggles with temptation, no self-induced guilt trips over having given in—things like goodness and kindness and celebration and joy will have their way day after day. We'll be in the constant presence of Jesus, and the ills of time will be no more. Plus, it will finally be payday! We'll receive reward for whatever good things we've done.

As I say, a pretty cool place to be. In fact, with all that heaven has going for it, you'd think I would be dying to go. Actually, I am dreading my arrival there, for one simple reason: the line at the door.

✦☙✦

Based on the number of Christ followers I know who *still* have yet to catch grace, here is how I envision my arrival at the pearly gates: Saint Peter greets me and says he's happy to escort me to where Jesus is welcoming each new resident. I'm nearly skipping, I'm so elated to see my Master face-to-face. We wander through quaint little neighborhoods, all shiny from golden streets, me waving at Abraham, Noah, Job, as we pass by various homes. Finally we get to the reception area. This is it—what I've been waiting for! Peter excuses himself and heads back to his post, while I turn and find ... a line.

The number of people snaking their way toward the front is incredible. It's worse than IKEA on opening day. I gently elbow the guy in front of me and ask, "How long you been waiting so far?"

I immediately realize it's a silly question, which he confirms with a subtle grin. "There's no time here, remember? But my guess? Coupla days."

✵

I crane an ear toward the front of the line, hoping to hear why it's taking so long, when I catch some middle-aged executive type giving a rundown of his entire life. "Well, for starters," I hear him say, "that pack of Bubble Yum they said I stole back when I was five? That was my brother Harry, God. You *know* I am more ethical than that."

A few yards ahead of me, a guy mutters, "Thanks a lot, Joe. How am I going to explain *that* one away?"

Joe continues. "Lord, now as far back as I can remember," he says, "I have always done the right thing. Well, except for the entire decade of my twenties. But I've *more* than made up for that. Take last week: I slowed at every school crosswalk, I helped that elderly lady get to her car, I returned the money when the cashier gave me too much change, and I refrained from cussing even *once*, even though my entire sales team let me down."

I start to get excited, thinking maybe he's done with his list of good works, but only until I hear him head back in time again, picking up with life in first grade. "And then that time during recess when the other boys teased her, *I* was the one who came to her defense ..."

Immeasurable hours pass by, and the man rambles on, trumpeting his grandest decisions and explaining away his every sin.

And then the next person in line gets a turn. But he's no better than the first guy, and slowly it begins to dawn on me that somehow everyone standing in front of me failed to ever catch the gift of grace. Now their only recourse is to enumerate their good deeds, while my only option is to wait. I will be tempted to shout from my place in line, "For the sake of the rest of us, if you never embraced the revelation of grace, could you just head to the back of the line?" But thinking it might be frowned upon to be impatient and huffy in heaven, I will bite my tongue and bide my "time."

⋊

By way of contrast, here is how quick the process will be for those of us who have accepted God's grace. We will approach the throne of our King and with all humility and deference say, "Father, I will never understand why you allowed me to be your son. But I am so grateful for our relationship, and for the grace that made it happen. You pursued me when I was still sinful, and you brought me into the fold. Any merit I have is unwarranted. All glory belongs to you. My only goal in this life was to be a grateful sheep and to follow my Shepherd all of my days."

Next!

I will be hip-deep in heaven's fun while people who never learned grace are still futilely rattling off their lists.

⋊

I don't know what is going on at your house these days, but at the Boyd house here lately, we're talking a lot about how to be grateful sheep. Quick to listen and easy to lead—that's our big family goal in life. No list making. No tracking of good deeds. Just ever-ready obedience to our Shepherd and ever-present joy over being his sheep. We want to keep our eyes trained on him, our ears attuned to him, our hands available to help. We want to make his name famous, give him all the glory, and show others how to come into the fold. We are the privileged people of his pasture—what more in life could we want?

Someday I am going to die. That's a safe bet, anyway. And when I do, my family will put me in a box and drop me into the ground in the Boyd burial plot in the woods of northwest Louisiana. They will load dirt on top of me and seal off my grave and pound a head-stone into the ground. And on that marker that is supposed to sum up my life, I hope it reads, "Here lies a grateful sheep."

This is my one ambition in life—to follow well with a grateful heart.

AFTERWORD

I n the late 1990s, I was serving as senior pastor of a small church
in Hereford, Texas, a city whose only claim to fame is as the beef
capital of the world. Pam and I had moved to Hereford from Amarillo, also located in the Texas Panhandle, and still maintained close
ties to leaders and congregants from our old church. My first year
in the senior pastor's seat, an Amarillo colleague called and invited
me to bring a group to their men's retreat. Our church of a hundred didn't have the resources to host our own conferences and
getaways, so I told him we would be happy to join them, and then
I got busy rallying our men. I thought the weekend would be a
nice bonding experience between the men of my new staff, a few
congregants, and me. What I didn't expect was that my own world
was about to get rocked.

A group of us arrived at Buena Vista, Colorado, prepared for
three days of enlightenment and fun. A guy nobody had heard of
took the platform and said he was going to devote the weekend to
the subject of grace. Perhaps a little prematurely, I sat back in my
chair, my self-possessed posture daring the speaker to teach me
something I didn't already know. I certainly didn't mean to seem
boastful; it's just that I was a pastor. Of course I understood grace.

By the end of day one, I was an absolute wreck. The more the
speaker talked, the more I realized that while I had been a devoted
Christ follower for ten full years, I had never grasped the gift of
God's grace. To my key leaders sitting on my left and on my right
in that retreat center's main room, I appeared leaderlike, in control,

and strong. But inside, there was a detonation happening, blowing up everything I thought I knew. There I was, the guy who was supposed to have all the answers, and all I could think about was the scores of questions now flooding my mind—deep spiritual questions I had no idea how to resolve.

I had lived as a spiritual orphan, forever trying to find his way home. And I had taken a long tangent into spiritual slavery, during which I had tried to garner God's favor with good works. But that weekend, I learned that I had never lived a day as God's cherished and chosen *son*.

✕

That men's retreat was thirteen years ago, and looking back, I recognize it for the defining moment that it was. I stood at a crossroads near the end of that three-day event: I could either brush past the experience and keep slaving away, or I could lean into the disruption and allow God to slowly transform my heart. Sitting in that little lodge, I said yes to God—to the *Father* I had never embraced. I told him I was committed to knowing him intimately, as a son knows his dad. And for the first time since I had surrendered to Christ, I felt bondage's chains simply melt away.

My steps along the path to sonship have been imperfect at best, but still, they have led me to Truth: God is near to his kids, and he is for us. We are accepted, approved, and adored. No amount of laudable effort can garner more favor than is already ours right now. And in the loving eyes of our Father, we will always have a place to call home.

NOTES

1. See *http://americanradioworks.publicradio.org/features/romania/a1.html*.
2. See *www.npr.org/templates/story/story.php?storyId=6089477*.
3. Max Lucado, *In the Grip of Grace* (Nashville: Nelson, 1996), 70.
4. The man I consider "my pastor," Pastor Robert Morris of Gateway Church in Southlake, Texas, coined this phrase. I am grateful to him for the loan.
5. R. T. Kendall, *How to Forgive Ourselves — Totally* (Lake Mary, Fla.: Charisma House, 2007), 17–30.
6. Ibid., 31.
7. Just to be sure, I had Karla call the elderly woman and verify that she had, in fact, intended to send us six thousand dollars in gold coins. The woman said, "Keep 'em! I've got my work cut out for me, making up for all this lost time."
8. Anne Lamott, *Traveling Mercies: Some Thoughts on Faith* (New York: Doubleday Anchor, 1999), 139.
9. Eugene Peterson, *The Pastor: A Memoir* (New York: HarperOne, 2011), 5.
10. Paul Tournier, *Guilt & Grace*, originally published as *Vraie ou Fausse Culpabilté* (San Francisco: Harper & Row, 1958), 17.
11. Helen H. Lemmel, 1922.
12. Yes, I know it should be "ridden." But when did this redneck ever claim to be an expert grammarian?
13. Marc Pittman, *Raising Cole: Developing Life's Greatest Relationship, Embracing Life's Greatest Tragedy* (Deerfield Beach, Fla.: Health Communications, 2004), 12.

14. Ibid.

15. Eugene Peterson, *Working the Angles: The Shape of Pastoral Integrity* (Grand Rapids: Eerdmans, 1989), 2.

16. Adapted from a Chinese proverb.

17. Tim Kimmel, *Grace-Based Parenting: Set Your Family Free* (Nashville: Nelson, 2004), 134.

18. See *http://comminfo.rutgers.edu/news/the-informers-and-the-meformers -study-reveals-two-types-of-twitter-users.html*.

19. Adam Hamilton, *24 Hours That Changed the World* (Nashville: Abingdon, 2009), 68.

20. Author's abridgment.

21. See *www.washingtonpost.com/blogs/early-lead/post/penn-state-scanda -sandusky-tells-costas-he-showered-with-boys-but-denies-abuse/2011 /11/15/gIQAvwUOON_blog.html* (accessed November 15, 2011).

22. See *www.thesecondmile.org/aboutUs.php* (accessed November 14, 2011).

23. Based on research from the National Center on Child Abuse and Neglect, a sanctioned arm of the federal government's Department of Health and Human Services.

24. See *http://online.wsj.com/article/SB10001424052748704409004576146 321725889448.html*: "Where Have All the Good Men Gone?" *Wall Street Journal,* online edition, 19 February 2011 (accessed 26 April 2012).

25. Paula McLain, "Like Family," excerpted in *Real Simple* (March 2011).